Number Symbolism

Ideas and forms in English Literature

Edited by John Lawlor

Professor of English, University of Keele

The English Georgic

A study in the development of a form

John Chalker

Number Symbolism

Christopher Butler

London
Routledge & Kegan Paul

First published in 1970
by Routledge & Kegan Paul Ltd.
Printed in Great Britain
by Ebenezer Baylis & Son Ltd.
The Trinity Press, Worcester, and London
Broadway House, 68–74 Carter Lane
London E.C.4
© *Christopher Butler 1970*

ISBN 0 7100 6766 6

to
Gillian

General Editor's Introduction

This series aims to explore two main aspects of literary tradition in English. First, the role of particular literary forms, with due emphasis on the distinctive sorts of application they receive at English hands; second, the nature and function of influential ideas, varying from large general conceptions evident over long periods to those concepts which are peculiar to a given age.

Each book attempts an account of the form or idea, and treats in detail particular authors and works rather than offering a general survey. The aim throughout is evaluative and critical rather than descriptive and merely historical.

J.L.

Contents

Preface

Never could error slip into number for its nature is
hostile thereto. Truth is the proper innate character of
number.

Stobaeus

Number exists before objects which are described by
number. The variety of sense objects merely recalls to the
soul the notion of number.

Plotinus

This book can claim to be only the briefest of introductions to a
very complex subject about which there still remains much to be
discovered. In it I have tried to present with a minimum of com-
ment a selection of the material which lies within an intellectual
tradition which runs from Pythagoras to the late Renaissance.
This tradition is now alien to us—within it, mathematics was
endowed with a mystic, allegorical significance. We have now
come to think of mathematics as the necessary substratum of the
physical sciences, the principal means by which we can discern a
rational order in physical phenomena. For many of the writers
whose work is described in this book, this would be simply to
remain at the level of the market place. These men all contributed
to a tradition with three main components. Firstly, a cosmological
science of creation according to numbers, in which 'God's plan'
was thought of as a mathematical one. Secondly, converging upon
the original Greek tradition, the discipline of Biblical exegesis, in
which the numbers in the Bible were held to have an allegorical
significance. Thirdly, and later still, we have a symbolic arith-
mology connected with magic, the occult, and astrology. These
three streams were industriously synthesized by Renaissance
writers. My aim is to show how the leading ideas of these systems

formed an integral part of Renaissance aesthetic, and influenced compositional methods in the arts, in all of which we may discern an 'allegory by numbers'. I conclude by describing some modern developments of the tradition, and by discussing the 'aesthetic of proportion' from the point of view of critical theory.

I am particularly indebted to Dr Alastair Fowler, for my original introduction to a fascinating topic, and for much helpful advice; to Professor Maren-Sofie Røstvig for emphasizing to me the importance of the tradition of Biblical exegesis; to Mr T. I. M. Beardsworth, for sharing his knowledge of Renaissance astronomy; to Dr Joan Wake and Sir Gyles Isham, for material concerning Sir Thomas Tresham; to Professor John Lawlor, the General Editor of this series, for much helpful advice concerning presentation; and to the Librarian and staff of Christ Church library for making available to me a surprisingly large number of Renaissance texts. The faults and errors which remain are entirely my own. My greatest debt is to my wife, who unstintingly encouraged, criticized, and typed this book, and to whom it is dedicated.

List of Abbreviations

De Gen. ad lit.	Augustine, *De Genesi ad litteram*
De Nuptiis	Capella, *De nuptiis Philologiæ et Mercurii*
De vera Relig.	Augustine, *De vera Religione*
Dox. Gr.	Diels, *Doxographi Graeci*
Enarr.	Augustine, *Enarratio[nes] in Psalmos*
JAAC	*Journal of Aesthetics and Art Criticism*
Leg. Alleg.	Philo, *Legum Allegoriae*
Num. Myst.	Bongo, *Numerorum Mysteria*
Post. An.	Aquinas, *Analytica Posteriora* (comm. on Aristotle)
Stud. Ren.	*Studies in the Renaissance*

One

The Greek Origins
of Number Symbolism

1 Pythagoras

The [Pythagoreans were] . . . the first to take up
mathematics . . . [and] thought its principles were the
principles of all things. Since of these principles numbers
are by nature the first, and in numbers they seemed to
see many resemblances to the things that exist and come
into being—more than in fire and earth and water (such
and such a modification of numbers being justice, another
being soul and reason, another being opportunity—and
similarly almost all things being universally expressible);
since, again, they saw that the modifications and ratios of
the musical scales were expressible in numbers; since,
then, all other things in their whole nature seemed to be
modelled on numbers, and numbers seemed to be the
first things in the whole of nature, they supposed the elements of number to be the elements of all things, and the
whole heaven to be a musical scale and a number. And
all the properties of numbers and scales which they
could show to agree with the attributes and parts and
the whole arrangement of the heavens, they connected
and fitted into their scheme; and if there was a gap any-
where, they readily made additions so as to make their
whole theory coherent.[1]

Thus Aristotle, in his *Metaphysica*, A.5. In his very compressed
account, these philosophical doctrines seem peculiar and inco-
herent; how can something like opportunity be a *number*? Why
are numbers the first principles, indeed the very elements,
of the things of nature? What sort of view of reality could the
Pythagoreans have, that would make the planetary system into a

I

musical scale? The ideas of Pythagoras are difficult to reconstruct in their totality, since we only know of him as he is reported by others, and notably by his hostile critic Aristotle; but they are the premises for the more sophisticated speculations of many later thinkers from Plato onwards.[2] My epigraph shows, I hope, just how speculative this thinking was. It is truly metaphysical in character, in that it attempts to give an account of the constitution of everything given to us in experience: 'Numbers seemed to be the first things in the whole of nature, they supposed the elements of number to be the elements of all things, and the whole heaven to be a musical scale and number.' In what follows I shall try to make a hypothetical reconstruction of Pythagoras' train of thought —to try to show how, as so often in philosophy, a single idea or 'intuition', really of limited scope, was generalized to explain phenomena far beyond its proper field—to show, in fact, how Pythagoras used number as the arch-synthesizer of cosmological knowledge.

For many people, there is a special fascination in playing with numbers in such a way as to reveal their structural properties. For instance, we may find that there are certain number-series which can be fitted into geometrical shapes. We can easily construct a progression of numbers, which when laid out as dots, are seen to be 'triangular' in nature. Thus:

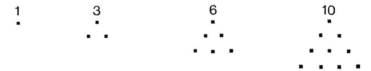

and so on. Since triangular numbers are built up by adding on successive rows of dots, it follows that they are sums of *arithmetical* progressions, which increase by one unit for each row. That is to say, a triangular number is the sum of successive numbers between which the difference is identical and constant. Thus the arithmetical progressions for triangular numbers are:

$$1 = 1$$
$$1 + 2 = 3$$
$$1 + 2 + 3 = 6$$
$$1 + 2 + 3 + 4 = 10$$

and so on. (In a *geometrical* progression each of the terms is related to the term next to it by a fixed ratio instead of a common difference, e.g. 3, 9, 27, 81, where each successive term is three times as great as the preceding one.) Since the Pythagoreans thought that One, the monad, was the principle of all number, containing in itself all the properties of other numbers, it counts as the first of the triangular numbers.

We also speak of 'square' numbers, 4, 9, 16, which can be represented by dots laid out in squares. These are also built up by the addition of arithmetical progressions, containing all the consecutive odd numbers from 1 upwards thus:

$$1 + 3 = 4 = 2^2$$
$$1 + 3 + 5 = 9 = 3^2$$
$$1 + 3 + 5 + 7 = 16 = 4^2$$
$$1 + 3 + 5 + 7 + 9 = 25 = 5^2$$

where the number of terms in each progression is the same as the number whose square results. Thus the square of 5 has 5 terms in its progression.

Pythagoras (580?–500? BC), his followers, and all early Greek mathematicians, thought of numbers in this geometrical way, probably using pebbles for the dots in my diagrams. As Sambursky points out, 'When we remember that the Greeks used to designate numbers by the letters of the alphabet—a system which completely concealed the laws of sequence in a series of numbers—the superiority of Pythagoras' method is at once evident.'[3]

When we call numbers 'figures' we are thus thinking in Pythagorean terms. For these thinkers 1 was a point, 2 (points) gave extension (the line), and 3 (points) could enclose a triangle, the first plane figure visible to sense, and thus the first *real* number. This led Plato to believe that the triangle must be the basis of all objects perceptible to the senses, and that surfaces are composed of triangles (cf. *Timaeus* 55–6). By the number 4 is signified the first solid, the pyramid or tetrahedron, composed of four triangular surfaces, with four apices. In the tenth chapter of *Theologumena Arithmetica* attributed to Iamblichus, we find a passage attributed to Speusippus, the son of Plato's sister Potone, who succeeded him in the Academy before Xenocrates, which says: 'the point is the first principle leading to magnitude, the line the second, surface third, and solid fourth.' He also says, 'one is a point, two a line, three a triangle and four a pyramid'. This can be diagrammatically represented:

By treating numbers geometrically, and by taking their geometrical properties as the properties of solids, that is as having extension, having a surface, and being of three dimensions, it was then possible to forget about this intermediate stage, which is merely reasoning by analogy, and to say that physical objects *were* numbers. We have thus made the first perplexing transition in Pythagorean thinking: we have seen how numbers could be thought of as things—so far, only as geometrical objects. But, as we shall see in discussing Plato in the next section, it is a very small jump further to say that below the level of normal sense discrimination, everyday objects are 'really' made up of these theoretical geometrical shapes. One has only to remember the way in which we can now think of a table as 'really' a conglomeration of atoms or molecules.

Pythagoras was led by the way in which he thought about numbers to make a discovery quite different from the identification of numbers with things. This discovery of his seemed to clinch the matter, and led him to speculate even further, this time about the relationship of objects within space. It was shown to be one of much more basic and far-reaching cosmological significance, upon which Plato himself builds. Pythagoras first stated the mathematical ratios involved in musical harmonic relationships. He was not concerned with harmony in our sense of simultaneously sounded notes in chords, or polyphony, but with those intervals which were most important in the tuning of the Greek musical scales, or modes. These were, for the Greek seven stringed lyre, the octave, the fifth, and the fourth—the tuning of the remaining three strings varying according to the type of scale required.[4] Pythagoras saw that this basic framework depended upon fixed and simple numerical ratios: 1:2 for the diapason, 3:2 for the fifth or diapente, 4:3 for the fourth or diatesseron, and 8:9 for the tone. These were the only intervals which the Greeks regarded as concordant. We do not know quite how Pythagoras discovered these ratios—it is doubtful whether he knew that these figures can represent the rate of vibration of a string, or of a stream of air in a pipe. There are apocryphal stories that he found out the ratios by suspending weights on strings or by hitting anvils with differently weighted hammers.[5]

It is nevertheless most likely that Pythagoras made his discovery on the Kanon or monochord, a single string with a movable bridge. Thus Pythagoras initiated the conception, of incalculable importance for later science, that qualitative differences in sense perception may be dependent upon mathematics. He also initiated the search, a part of which will be documented in this book, for objective standards of beauty. For if the consonances that please us depend upon simple mathematical ratios, ought we not to bow to these mathematical laws in constructing musical works of art?[6]

The Pythagoreans were so impressed by their harmonic discoveries, that they believed they had come across the basic laws of the universe. The very simplicity of the ratios, their containment within the all important and powerful decad, which brought all things back to the unity they reverenced ($1 + 2 + 3 + 4 = 10$), and their use in the generation of figures, as shown above, must have helped to convince them of this. They generalized their knowledge of the relationship between music and numbers, and made it the basis of any true knowledge of the soul, and of the 'cosmos'.

Pythagoras thus came to be most famous for his conception of the 'music of the spheres'—an attempt to explain the whole plan of the universe by reference to his basic discovery. This was the view that the physical bodies in the heavens must be moving so rapidly that they emit a sound (as happens when we swish a stick through the air, though as celestial bodies they would of course emit a less mundane sound than this). It seemed clear to the Pythagoreans (as reported by Aristotle, *De Caelo* II, 9) that the spatial intervals between the seven planets and the sphere of the fixed stars would correspond to the mathematical ratios for the notes of the octave in the diatonic scale, and that the sounds emitted by them would also so correspond. In fact this doctrine cannot be traced directly to Pythagoras. The first exposition of it in Greek literature occurs in Plato's myth of Er at the end of the *Republic*, where he tells us that 'the spindle of the cosmos turns on the knees of Necessity. Upon each of its circles stood a Siren who was carried round with its movement, uttering the concords of a single scale'. Apart from this enigmatic account by Plato and the expository one of Aristotle[7] the chief descriptions of the 'music of the spheres' date from the Graeco-Roman period, and especially from Macrobius and the *Somnium Scipionis*.

The Pythagoreans not only thus speculated upon the mathematical relationships between the observable planetary bodies. Their reverence for number, particularly the number 10, which not only contained the numbers of harmony but was also thought of as Unity, led them to postulate a 'counter-earth' or central fire, round which the earth moved, but which was never visible, because the earth's populated areas were always turned away from it. They thus made up the number of the planetary bodies to the desired unifying number, 10 (counter-earth, earth, moon, Mercury, Venus, sun, Mars, Jupiter, Saturn, sphere of the fixed stars).

Aristotle comments on this very scathingly:

> They further construct another earth, in opposition to ours, which they call the 'counter-earth', as they do not in regard to phenomena seek for their reasons and causes, but forcibly make the phenomena fit their opinions and preconceived notions. . . . As ten is the perfect number they maintain that there must be ten bodies moving in the heavens, and as only nine are visible they make the counter-earth the tenth.
>
> *(De Caelo, 293a).*

This criticism is of course deserved; but nevertheless the Pythagoreans made a great advance in astronomical thinking by devising an astronomical system which was a working *model*. This was a considerable improvement upon their inheritance from the Babylonians, who were really only concerned to observe and compute the separate positions of major planets in the sky and were not much interested in what the planets did in between those positions, or what their three-dimensional relationships to each other were. Thus the Pythagorean scheme could have been a basis, ultimately correctable by observation, for a mathematical explanation of physical processes, such as lies at the basis of modern science. However, as Sambursky points out,[8] Plato's later doctrine of Ideas ensured that these systems remained objects of the religious contemplation of Ideal Forms, so that they were not used as schemata for practical empirical investigation. Just as the cosmos is ordained according to number, so, according to Pythagoras, the soul which contemplates it must be. The soul itself is a harmony. All nature is akin, and like is known by like. As we grow in knowledge of the order of the cosmos so we also order and cultivate the divine element in ourselves. Thus Aristotle in his *Politics*:

> There seems to be in us a sort of affinity to musical modes and rhythms, which makes many philosophers say that the soul is a harmonia, others that it possesses harmonia.[9]

Remnants of this way of talking still survive perhaps in our talk of 'well tempered people', or of administering a 'tonic' for illness. But the main point is that here again the musical analogy, the undeniable effect of music upon the mind of the hearer, was, not surprisingly, generalized to describe the effects on the mind of contemplation of order in physical phenomena, which latter were themselves believed to proceed according to musical laws.

This Pythagorean reverence for number led them to endow individual numbers with symbolic qualities. For instance Justice *was* the number 4, on the ground that justice essentially involved a recriprocal relationship between persons, and that reciprocity was embodied in a square number.

> Because they assumed, as a defining property of justice, requital or equality, and found this to exist in numbers, therefore they said that justice was the first square number; for in every kind the first instance of things having the same formula had in their opinion the best right to the name. This number some said was 4, as being the first square, divisible into equal parts and in every way equal, for it is twice 2. Others, however, said that it was 9, the first square of an odd number, namely 3 multiplied by itself.
>
> Opportunity, on the other hand, they said, was 7, because in nature the times of fulfilment with respect to birth and maturity go in sevens. Take man for instance. He can be born after seven months, cuts his teeth after another seven, reaches puberty about the end of his second period of seven years, and grows a beard at the third. . . .[10]

Certain other numbers were especially reverenced for their factorizing possibilities—for instance 'perfect' numbers, which are the sum of their divisors exclusive of themselves (their aliquot parts), such as six ($= 1 + 2 + 3$), and 28, the second perfect number, which was also thought to be astrologically significant. By the same token there were 'deficient' numbers, for instance 14, the sum of whose factors is less than 14, and 'abundant' ones, like 12, the sum of whose factors is more than 12. There were also 'circular' numbers which perpetually reproduce their last digit when raised to their powers, for instance 5 and 6. (9 was also thought to be circular after the introduction of Arabic notation, because however often multiplied it continually reproduces itself in the sum of its digits.)

These ways of regarding numbers are clearly symbolic in the basic sense that they use mathematical concepts to recall to mind essentially non-mathematical objects, properties or processes. Although the idea that abstractions like justice and opportunity were embodiments of number seemed absurd even to Aristotle,[11] the Pythagorean conception stands at the beginning of a never-ending search for analogical properties of individual numbers (for instance reciprocity), and for number structures underlying significant human experiences (for instance the observations that went to confirm that 7 was the number of opportunity). Astrological numbers are also of this latter type, as in the correlation of the moon's cycle of 28 days with the menstruation cycle. This type of analogical and structural symbolism diverges quite clearly from the theological and scientific (astronomical) stream of Pythagorean thought, in which numbers are thought of as the essential modifying framework, which organizes the physical world as we perceive it.

The most reverenced numbers, however, were 1, 2, 3, and 4. A book could be written upon the history of the symbolism of these numbers alone. The legend grew up that the Pythagorean initiates swore an oath by the sacred tetraktys,

the triangular representation of the number 10 considered as

1 + 2 + 3 + 4. These initiates constituted a secret society whose aim was ethical salvation. As part of their initiation they were vowed to silence for three years, and thus during the Renaissance the number 1095 (= 3 × 365) was believed to be the number of silence. They thought of One, the monad, as good and divine, and of the dyad as an evil daimon breaking away from the divine One, thus representing the plurality and change of the material world. Here Pythagorean thinking about number came to reflect their dualistic religious thinking. This aspect, as we shall see, appealed strongly to the Manichaean Neo-Pythagoreans of the early centuries A.D., whom St Augustine initially found so convincing.

The reverence for the tetraktys in particular proved to be one of the most imaginatively compelling aspects of Pythagoreanism. It was treated as a key to the understanding of the whole of life. Theon of Smyrna, writing in the first century A.D., in his chapter 'On the tetraktys and the Decad' enumerates ten sets of four things that the tetraktys was held to symbolize:

Numbers: 1, 2, 3, 4.
Magnitudes: point, line, surface, solid.
Simple Bodies: fire, air, water, earth.
Figures of simple bodies: pyramid, octahedron, icosa-
    hedron, cube.
Living Things: seed, growth in length, in breadth, in
    thickness.
Societies: man, village, city, nation.
Faculties: reason, knowledge, opinion, sensation.
Seasons of the Year: spring, summer, autumn, winter.
Ages: infancy, youth, manhood, age.
Parts of the human being: body and the three parts of soul.

This numerological method of categorizing experience proved so popular, that when Cornelius Agrippa came to write his *De Occulta Philosophia* in 1510, he lists no less than 31 tetrads in his 'Scale of the Number Four'. These attempts to classify basic elements of experience do reflect a genuine philosophical concern, that is to say they seek generality in demonstrating how we unify our experience. But the mistake that Theon and others conditioned by the Pythagorean world view were led to make, lay in not realizing that any basic categories in our experience must arise from the way we actually do think about it, that is from language,

and not from number. But, as we shall shortly see, the arithmologists believed that God himself thought of his creation, indeed
thought it up, arithmetically, and they were more theologically
motivated to share the thought of God, than to make philosophical
sense of everyday experience. The Pythagoreans, instead of saying
that things could be conveniently described by means of number,
took the ontological leap into saying that they *were* essentially
number. Nevertheless their desire to interpret nature in terms of
number relations does lie at the basis of the scientific doctrine of
our own day, that nature, from physical to sociological, must
be studied quantitatively. The belief in mathematics is similar,
although we tend to use mathematical methods for prediction and
control, whereas the Greeks tied mathematics more strictly to
theory and contemplation. Their mathematics and geometry are
essentially static. Their metaphysic led them to see the universe in
terms of an arithmetical analogy. These doctrines, as we shall see,
are at the root of much subsequent speculation which starts from
the assumption that the universe must be ordered in a mathematically harmonious way. The influence of Pythagoras remains
strong until the final divergence of mathematical metaphysics
from the mathematics used quite neutrally to record observations.

Why did the Pythagoreans place such a huge reliance upon
mathematics? Perhaps a clue is provided by the following quotation from Philolaus, who came over from Italy and settled in
Thebes around 460 B.C. He is the first written authority on
Pythagoreanism.[12]

> One must study the activities and the essence of Number,
> in accordance with the power existing in the Decad
> (Ten-ness); for it (the Decad) is great, complete, all
> achieving, and the origin of divine and human life and
> its Leader . . .
> For the nature of number is the cause of recognition,
> able to give guidance and teaching to every man in what
> is puzzling and unknown. For none of existing things
> would be clear to anyone either in themselves or in their
> relationship to one another, unless there existed Number
> and its essence. But in fact Number, fitting all things
> into the soul through sense perception, makes them
> recognizable and comparable with one another . . . in

that Number gives them body and divides the different relationships of things. . . .

And you may see the nature of Number and its power at work not only in supernatural and divine existences but also in all human activities and words every where, both throughout all technical production and also in music.

Falsehood can in no way breathe on Number; for Falsehood is inimical and hostile to its nature, whereas Truth is related and in close natural union with the race of Number.[13]

2 *Plato*

Plato in his *Timaeus* continues the Pythagorean tradition.[14] For Plato, as for Pythagoras before him, true morality is an order and harmony of the soul; and the soul mirrors on the natural plane the Soul of the World. The cosmos is itself a God, a living creature with soul in body and reason in soul (cf. *Timaeus* 29D–30C). Upon the chaotic materials of a divine and unique world, the mythical creating Demiurge goes to work. The basic cosmology of the *Timaeus* is arithmological, and highly systematized.

In this dialogue we have the first Greek account of a divine creation, together with a rational account of a number of natural processes, an account which was highly influential for many centuries, and easily assimilated to the book of *Genesis* by Christian thinkers. It is a religiously motivated teleological account of the physical and superlunary celestial worlds, on the analogy not of human or animal procreation, but of the constructive activity of a master craftsman or Demiurge (who is, however, not an object of worship). In the early part of the work (the 53 sections available in the Middle Ages, in Chalcidius' translation), Plato is basically concerned to tell us: (a) how the Demiurge in the beginning divides an indeterminate chaos of space into the four elements of fire, air, water and earth, by forming them out of geometrical solids; (b) what proportions the Demiurge chose for the World's Body; (c) how he disposed the celestial bodies in space.

This myth of the creator working to a plan helps to account for the intelligibility of the world of Becoming as we know it, accounts for its quality as a system. There were two main problems for

Plato here; to determine the structure of matter, and to explain the obviously regular and observable movements of the heavenly bodies. The known motions for which Plato had to account were:

(a) the diurnal rotation of all heavenly bodies from east to west.
(b) the 'wandering' of the sun, moon and planets through the signs of the Zodiac (in the fixed stars) from west to east.
(c) retrogradation.

This latter problem was the most embarrassing one that the early astronomers had to face. The planets appear to turn back in their courses for a period, and then carry on in their usual eastward motion. This seems to be a check to the supposedly immutable and eternal circular motions of the heavenly bodies, and makes it impossible to describe the physical path of a planet through the sky as a perfect circle along which the planet moves at a constant speed. I describe some attempts to solve the problem in a later chapter.

The exposition of parts of the *Timaeus* which follows is highly selective. I shall be concerned with the mathematical ideas used by Plato, and not for instance with the status of his account as a creation myth, or the adequacy of his astronomy to the observations available at his time.

(a) The Body of the World

In the *Timaeus* 31B–32C Plato wishes to demonstrate that the world is a unique copy of a perfect and eternal model, that it is made up of four primary bodies, and that the Demiurge has fixed the quantities of these bodies in certain definite proportions:

So God, when he began to put together the body of the universe, made it of fire and earth. (So that it should be both visible and solid.) But it is not possible to combine two things properly without a third to act as a bond to hold them together. And the best bond is one that effects the closest unity between itself and the terms it is combining; and this is best done by a continued geometrical proportion (ἀναλογια).[15]

Plato is assuming what is obvious, that physical bodies are locked together in the universe. Granted that mathematics provides the plan on which this was done, one has to look for a numerical sequence in which the numbers are mutually interrelated in the 'tightest' and most satisfactory way. Thus Plato, like Pythagoras, is treating numbers as if they were physical things. If numbers can be made to bind together in some mathematical sense, then that is also the way in which observable physical objects, made of the four elements, are held together. This is achieved best by three rather than by two numbers—the mean number providing the 'lock'. All primary bodies (elements) are solids and therefore must be represented by 'solid' numbers (that is, cubes). Between two square numbers there is one mean proportional number; between two cubes there are two mean proportional numbers. The way the numbers interlock can perhaps be shown best by taking a more simple sequence, say 2, 4, 6, 8. Then 2:4::4:8, and 8:4::4:2 and 4:2::8:4. These numbers have, as we see, several satisfying inter-relations. An even better though far more complicated result can be achieved with the appropriate cubed numbers. (Cornford discusses these in his commentary, p. 45 ff.)

With one middle term in such sequences then, we have only a plane surface, but with two mean terms between the separate numbers, the four numbers all symbolizing elements, we achieve solidity.

> So God placed water and air between fire and earth, and made them as far as possible proportional to one another; so that air is to water as water is to earth; and in this way he bound the earth into a visible and tangible whole.

All these elements, Plato says, are in concord or amity.[16] Putting them in continued geometrical proportion solved another problem —as Cornford tells us:

> Empedocles had made his four elements equal in amount, but since his time it had been realized that the world was much larger than had been supposed. Since the heavenly bodies are composed mostly of fire, it is natural to suppose that the total volume of fire is much greater than that of earth. The largest number would then represent the volume of fire, the smallest that of earth.[17]

Plato was not of course concerned to say how *much* there was of each element in the universe. He only believed they must be in some definite rational, designed proportion, which would prevent any possible dissolution due to internal disharmony.

At 33B Plato argues that the world's body must be spherical, since this is the most uniform shape within which any equilateral polygon can be inscribed; and further, the axial rotation of the whole universe can then symbolize the movement of Reason. It is not clear why axial rotation should have this symbolic connotation. Presumably in Plato's theological conception the lack of movement in any linear direction would symbolize the 'self containment' and immutability of a reasonable World Soul.

(b) The World Soul

The World Soul is described as a long strip, with a mathematical structure. This strip is cut up into narrower strips which are used to produce the movements of the heavenly bodies. These movements are on two cross-wise strips, one, the circle of 'the Same' for the fixed stars, the other, the circle of 'the Different' for the planets.[18] Thus this latter circle is in turn subdivided into seven, one circular band, of varying size, for the orbit of each planet.

This seems both a peculiar and an unlikely model for astronomical movements. It seems unlikely because we may forget that for the Greeks the soul as self-moving is the ultimate cause of motion. As such the soul, which we think of as an immaterial ghostlike thing, is for Plato more akin to a mechanism, like an armillary sphere. Happily we need not be concerned with the cruces of interpretation in this passage.[19] What is important for our purposes is to realize that for Plato the soul of the world, when divided into its strips, is divided according to a particular numerical series. This is 1, 2, 3, 4, 8, 9, 27. Ancient commentators pointed out that this can be arranged into a diagram, the Platonic Lambda, so called because of its resemblance to the Greek letter.

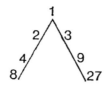

The reason for stopping these numerical progressions at the cube, is that the cube symbolizes body in three dimensions. There have to be two series because Pythagorean theory demanded that the odd numbers should be represented as well as the even.

Most importantly, Plato treats these numbers as if, when in continuous series, they defined a musical scale. Cornford (p. 71) shows how harmonic and arithmetical means can be inserted between the numbers of this series to give a scale with intervals of a tone or semitone, over a compass of four octaves and a major sixth. The wide range of this shows that Plato was not concerned with practical musical possibilities, but that the World Soul yet consists of a '*harmonia*'. This series is perhaps used later to define the actual sizes of the planetary orbits (cf. 36D).

(c) Music and the Soul

A very important passage of the *Timaeus* for our purposes, but one that is rarely commented on (it is passed over completely by Cornford), is the passage at 47Aff, concerning music and the soul.

> . . . the sight of day and night, the months and returning years, the equinoxes and solstices, has caused the invention of number, given us the notion of time, and made us inquire into the nature of the universe; thence we have derived philosophy . . . we should see the revolutions of intelligence in the heavens and use their untroubled courses to guide the troubled revolutions in our own understanding, which are akin to them . . . all audible musical sound is given us for the sake of harmony, which has motions akin to the orbits in our soul and which, as anyone who makes intelligent use of the arts knows, is not to be used, as is commonly thought, to give irrational pleasure, but as a heaven-sent ally in reducing to order and harmony any disharmony in the revolutions within us.

This reminds us that the ultimate aim of philosophy is a moral one, the attainment of a certain kind of life, the tuning of the soul in harmony with the universe. Arithmologists in the tradition to be discussed in this book believed that their speculations would 'double back' so to speak, for the good of their souls. (Rather as the alchemists sought the transmutation of the self, as much as that of base metal, into gold.) Thus the inner life of man can be musicalized. Compare Plato's remark in the *Phaedo* (60C) that philosophy is μεγιστη μουσικη. This passage from the *Timaeus* also takes its place in a long tradition of medical belief, that music and the arts generally are of therapeutic use. I cannot resist anticipating later discussion by quoting this anecdote from Fulke Greville, who recalls that Sir Philip Sidney, on his death bed, called for music

> to fashion and enfranchise his heavenly soul unto that everlasting harmony of angels, whereof these concords are a kind of terrestrial echo . . . and in this . . . orb of contemplation, he blessedly went on, within a circular motion, to the end of all flesh.

In this, as in so much else, Sidney was a good Platonist.[20]

(d) Creation and the Regular Solids

The *Timaeus* has a fresh starting point at 47E—the theme is now the Demiurge's conquest of chaos, and construction of the primary (geometrical) bodies, which are then assigned to the four elements and the cosmos as a whole.

The 'Receptacle' of Space is 'qualified' by the main characters of fire, air, water, earth. Of these four there are independently real Forms, on the same general grounds that make it necessary to believe in any Forms whatsoever.

The four elements in Chaos had something of their proper character, yet they were in the

> disorganized state to be expected of anything which God has not touched, and his first step when he set about reducing them to order was to give them a definite pattern of shape and number.

Thus the Demiurge constructs the four elements as regular solids. Since all solid figures are bounded by planes, and since the most elementary plane figure is the triangle, two types of triangle are chosen as the basic constituents (building blocks) of those solid bodies which are later on to be severally assigned to the four elements. Three elements can be transformed into each other (for instance water into air by heating) so they are made from the same sorts of triangle, the scalene, with the lengths of the sides in the proportions 1, 2, 3, and angles of 60°, 30°, and 90°. The fourth, non-transformable element, earth, is made up of the other type of triangle, the isosceles, with sides 1,1 and 2 (53C–55C).[21] There still remains (55C) a fifth construction 'which God used for arranging the constellations on the whole heaven.'

Milton's God, under the suggestively Platonic title, 'Work-Maister', first conquers chaos by dividing it into four elements, just as the Demiurge does; and the use of the phrase 'ethereal quintessence of Heaven' suggests that Milton had in mind Plato's use of the fifth regular solid for the sphere of the constellations:

> Confusion heard his voice, and wild uproar
> Stood rul'd, stood vast infinitude confin'd;
> Till at his second bidding darkness fled,
> Light shon, and order from disorder sprung:
> Swift to their several Quarters hasted then
> The cumbrous Elements, Earth, Flood, Air, Fire,
> And this Ethereal quintessence of Heaven
> Flew upward, spirited with various forms,
> That round orbicular, and turnd to starrs
> Numberless, as thou seest, and how they move . . .
>
> (III, 710–719)

By putting triangles together in various ways, like a child playing with bricks, Plato ends up with the cube, the octahedron, the pyramid, and the icosahedron. He continues (55D):

> We must proceed to distribute the figures whose origins we have just described between fire, earth, water, and air. Let us assign the cube to earth; for it is the most immobile of the four bodies and the most retentive of shape, and these are characteristics that must belong to the figure with most stable faces. . . .

Similarly the smallest, most mobile and most sharp and penetrating figure (the pyramid) is assigned to fire. The least mobile of the four eligible figures (the icosahedron) is assigned to water, and the intermediate one (the octahedron) to air.

17

The fifth figure, the dodecahedron, cannot be constructed out of the basic triangles. Since it approaches the sphere in volume it is associated with the sphere of the heavens. Plato supposes it was used for arranging the constellations. How, we are not told.

The four shapes are chosen for the elements simply because they are 'the best'. They are clearly not the actual shapes of observable particles of water, etc. But Plato would say that the observable is an imperfect copy of the ideal type, which belongs to the intelligible world of mathematics.

My account here is extremely simplified. There are many problems arising out of this rather obscure text which I have left untouched. The reader is referred to Cornford and Taylor for discussion of these. My main aim here has been to bring before the reader those parts of Plato's *Timaeus* which contributed most to later number symbolism, for the *Timaeus* was an immensely influential text. Klibansky provides the following authoritative account:

> . . . there was hardly a mediaeval library of any standing which had not a copy of Chalcidius' version and some-times also a copy of the fragment translated by Cicero. Although these facts are well known, their significance for the history of ideas has perhaps not been sufficiently grasped by historians. The *Timaeus* with its attempted synthesis of the religious teleological justification of the world and the rational exposition of creation was, throughout the earlier Middle Ages, the starting point and guide for the first groping efforts towards a scientific cosmology.[22]

In our brief study of Pythagoras and Plato we have uncovered the fundamental assumptions of thinkers in what I shall call the arithmological or numerological tradition. These men inherited from the Greeks a profound reliance upon mathematics as an aid in thinking about the world philosophically—for they thought of mathematics as a specially privileged, truth-telling language. Even more important, mathematics could be used to synthesize knowledge. We have seen how those proportions which underlay Greek music, were supposed to be the very same as those which underlay the structure of the cosmos as a whole; and how Plato in his theory of matter, builds it of the most perfect geometrical forms he can think of, the regular solids, since only these are worthy of the creator. Here we see being introduced, an idea of immense importance for Hebrew and Christian theology from the Jew Philo through the Church Fathers to the astronomer Kepler: the idea of God as a being who in his creation proceeded *more geometrico*. The ideas of Pythagoras and Plato proved to be so influential largely because these mathematical ideas were brought into so many spheres of knowledge. As Spitzer reminds us, in the *Timaeus*: 'the world soul (a religious concept) the regulation of the cosmos (a concept of physics), world harmony (a musical concept) and the soul of man (a psychological concept) are fused. . . .'[23] This Greek appreciation of the order of the world was not simply religious and scientific, but also aesthetic. It arose from a strong belief in the beautiful order of creation, in a harmonized world-scheme, one which it is satisfying to contemplate. As Plato tells us in the *Republic* (525B), mathematics: 'draws the soul upwards . . . never allowing it to offer for discussion mere collections of visible or tangible bodies.' That is, it is indispensable as an aid to the purely philosophical appreciation of the world of Forms, in that it removes the soul from sense-knowledge and prepares it for philosophical dialectic.

In this chapter I have tried to introduce (with some unavoidable injustice to the complexity of the thought of Pythagoras and Plato), some of the 'technical concepts' of numerological thinking which, we will find, form the main core of a tradition of thought which extends from Plato to the late Renaissance period. The concepts of the 'World Soul' (and hence of a subtly animistic universe), of a mathematically ordered creation (which lays the foundation for scientific study), and so on, will be reported and commented on again and again, by the Fathers of the Church, encyclopaedists, astronomers and astrologers, philosophers and magicians, and put to some very strange uses, far removed from the original Greek intention.

In the following chapter, then, we make a jump in time to the immediately pre-Christian era, to see how a second, equally powerful stream of thought—that based on the Bible—managed to combine with the Greek one.

Notes

[1] Aristotle, *Metaphysica* A.5 985b (Ross, vol. VIII).

[2] It should be noted that it is not possible to attribute all of the doctrines discussed in this chapter to the historical Pythagoras. His sect kept laws of secrecy; and when his doctrines became more broadcast in the revival of Pythagoreanism which began at about the time of Cicero, and continued until the rise of the Neo-Platonic school in the third century A.D., any view of the right temper was attributed to him. For instance Iamblichus often attributes doctrines to Pythagoras himself, when 'the Pythagoreans' is all that stands in his source.

[3] *The Physical World of the Greeks* (London, 1956), ch. II, p. 27.

[4] Cf. Burnet, *Early Greek Philosophy I* (London, 1930), pp. 45–9.

[5] It became traditional to believe that this was how Pythagoras made his discovery; cf. e.g. Stahl, ed., *The Somnium Scipionis of Macrobius* (1953), p. 187 n6, or, for the Renaissance, Gafurio, *Theoria Musicae* (1492).

[6] Cf. Plato, *Republic*, 531A: they 'look for numerical relationships in audible concords'. Richard L. Crocker, *JAAC* (1963–4), argues that Pythagoras' discovery is still basically valid. So does Ernest Ansermet, *Les fondements de la musique dans la conscience humaine* (Geneva, 1961)

[7] Cf. *De Caelo*, 290 b 12ff, and 291 a 8.

[8] Op. cit., p. 30; cf. p. 43.

[9] 1340 b. 18. Cf. Plato, *Phaedo*, 86 b; Aristotle, *De Anima*, 407 b 27.

[10] Alexander of Aphrodisias (a commentator on Aristotle) in his *In Metaphysica*, 38:10 quoted by Guthrie, *History of Greek Philosophy I* (Cambridge, 1962), pp. 303–4.

[11] Cf. *Metaphysica*, 1093 a 1; 985 b 29; 1078 b 21; and 990 a 18.

[12] According to Iamblichus, *Vita Pythag.*, 199.

[13] Quoted from K. Freeman, *Ancilla to the Presocratic Philosophers* (Cambridge, 1948), p. 75.

[14] A. E. Taylor believed that the *Timaeus* basically represented the views of a fifth-century Pythagorean and thus did not represent Plato's mature ideas. Cornford, *Plato's Cosmology* (London, 1937), argues against him that this is not so, for Aristotle was with Plato in the Academy when he composed the *Timaeus*, and does not use it as a source for fifth-century Pythagoreanism.

[15] Quoted from the Lee translation (Penguin Books, 1965), p. 43.

[16] A reference to the *philia* of Empedocles system (Cornford, p. 44). The 'four of amity' was important in Renaissance thought and especially in Spenser, cf. A. D. S. Fowler, *Spenser and the Numbers of Time* (London, 1964), p. 24ff.

[17] Cornford, op. cit., p. 51.

[18] This is the nucleus of the ancients' concept of the 'two-sphere universe', which is described exhaustively in Kuhn, *The Copernican Revolution* (New York, 1959), ch. 1.

[19] On which see Cornford, op. cit., pp. 59–66.

[20] Fulke Greville, *The Life of Sir Philip Sidney* (London, 1652) in *Works* ed. Grosart (1870), IV, p. 139. The passage is quoted by G. L. Finney in her 'Music, a Book of Knowledge in Renaissance England', *Stud. Ren.* VI (1959).

21 Lee, op. cit., p. 74 fn., remarks that 'the exclusion of earth from the cycle of transformation seems to be due solely to the assignation to it of the cube, and not to be based on any facts of observation'. There are many problems as to the relative sizes and construction of the triangles, see Cornford, p. 210 ff. Stephen Toulmin and June Whitfield produce a very ingenious theory in *The Architecture of Matter* (Penguin Books, 1965), pp. 82–9.
22 R. Klibansky, *The Continuity of the Platonic Tradition* (London, Warburg Institute, 1939), pp. 28–9.
23 *Classical and Christian Ideas of World Harmony* (Baltimore, 1963), p. 11.

Two

The Early Medieval Period: Biblical Exegesis and World Schemes

1 The Bible

Philo Judaeus (*c.* 30 B.C.–A.D. 50), an Alexandrian Jew, and the first major thinker of this period, attempted a reconciliation between Hellenistic and Jewish thought, notably between the supposedly Mosaic account of creation in *Genesis*, and the Pythagorean-inspired, number-symbolic account. According to him, it is only by allegorical exegesis that we can penetrate the literal words of *Genesis*, and come to a true estimate of the matter. Thus he explains that God created the world in six days,

> because for things coming into existence there was need of order. Order involves number, and among numbers by the laws of nature the most suitable to productivity is 6, for if we start with 1 it is the first perfect number, being equal to the product of its factors (i.e. 1 × 2 × 3) as well as made up of the sum of them (i.e. 1 + 2 + 3), its half being 3, its third part 2, its sixth part 1. We may say that it is in its nature both male and female, and is a result of the distinctive power of either. For among things that are, it is the odd that is male, and the even female. Now of odd numbers 3 is the starting point, and of even numbers 2, and the product of these two is 6. For it was requisite that the world, being most perfect of all things that have come into existence, should be constituted in accordance with a perfect number, namely six; and, in as much as it was to have in itself beings that sprang from a coupling together, should receive the impress of a mixed number, namely the first in which odd and even

were combined, one that should contain the essential principle both of the male that sows and of the female that receives the seed.[1]

This remarkable passage has a speciously attractive logic—but it operates basically in terms of symbolic analogy. Certainly, in a sense, we order things according to number; so may God have done. But it is *we* who decide that 6 shall be called a 'perfect number'; it is not a peculiar kind of law of nature that this should be so. By symbolizing 3 as male, and 2 as female, Philo also introduces an aura of the older, more literally procreative creation myths. He then equivocates on the meaning of 'perfect', which at one point has a relatively technical mathematical meaning of 'a number equal to the product of its factors exclusive of itself' (i.e. the number 6), and at the next means 'the best conceivable' (i.e. the universe, created in six days). But these analogical extensions of meaning were, to the exegetes of our period, not slippery equivocations of the meanings of terms that ought to be kept philosophically pure, but rather evidence for the miraculous interconnectedness of things, which had number as their essence, and of the divine plan which used all intellectual traditions in its providential workings towards the venerated truth. Hence the revolutionary 'discovery' of Pythagorean elements in the supposedly Mosaic Pentateuch. This was the view that Pythagoras' and Plato's insights had really been derived from their knowledge of Moses and the Prophets. Compare also St Augustine, *City of God* (VIII, 11) where he argues that the similarity of Plato to *Genesis* shows that Plato was indebted to the Mosaic narrative. So persistent was this view, that Mosaic Pythagorean mysteries were still being revealed as late as the seventeenth century, for instance in Robert Fludd's *Philosophia Moysaica* (1638).

What are the motives for Philo's type of exegesis? Why should the story of *Genesis* be thus conflated with Greek number symbolism? Philo was a proselytizing Alexandrian Jew, acutely aware of the problems of making the Old Testament seem both superior to Greek myth, and equal to Greek philosophy. Professor Chadwick acutely summarizes Philo's predicament and its solution:

If one dismissed as childish legends the flood of Deucalion or the Aloadae piling Pelion upon Ossa to reach heaven, what should one say about Noah, or the tower of Babel?

Allegorical interpretation, as long practised by exegetes
of Homer and systematized by the Stoics, especially on
the basis of the etymologies of proper names, offered a
way of liberation and modernization.[2]

Thus we have to view the passage quoted from Philo as part of an
attempt to show that the Mosaic Pentateuch narrative could be
seen as taking account of all that was best in Greek theology,
science, and ethics. It was not enough to aver an historical relationship between Pythagoras and Moses—the Hebrew texts
themselves (the Greek versions of which Philo accepted as equally
divinely inspired) had to yield the desired, more civilized meaning. Thus Philo attempts to fuse the sternly monotheistic ethical
working relationship of Jehovah with his Chosen People, with the
transcendental philosophy of Platonism. The danger of numerological thinking in this sphere was of course that God would cease
to be a Person and become a Number. For Philo conceives of God
in the Pythagorean fashion as the One or Monad and yet we are
rather surprisingly assured that the One True God is 'beyond the
monad'.[3] The great gain for Philo was that he could see, as the
passage quoted on *Genesis* amply illustrates, this created sensible
world as in some way a reflection of an immanent intelligible
order. This eternal intelligible realm is that of the Platonic Ideas
which are God's thoughts, of which the prime examples are in the
mathematical plan involved in the order and disposition of
Creation.[4] It is not surprising that the saying 'aut Plato philonissat
aut Philo platonissat', became popular among the Greek Fathers
of the Church. And thus, as Professor Chadwick reminds us, 'the
history of Philo's influence lies in Christianity, not in Judaism.'[5]
However, the final, patristic, seal of approval was given to
numerological thinking by one of the greatest and most influential
of the Church Fathers, St Augustine. In his *Civitas Dei*, in a
passage also on the six days of creation as corresponding to the
perfect number six, he says:

> We must not despise the science of numbers, which, in
> many passages of Holy Scripture, is found to be of
> eminent service to the careful interpreter. Neither has it
> been without reason numbered among God's praises
> 'thou hast ordered all things in number and measure
> and weight'.[6]

This last tag from the Book of Solomon, was a vital link between the Old Testament, that is the Hebrew tradition, and the *Timaeus*. Indeed Augustine explicitly recalls, in *Civitas Dei* XII, 18, that Plato represented God as constructing the world on numerical principles. A further quotation from the Book of Wisdom (19:17) was commonly held to echo the Timaean ordering of the universe upon musical principles: 'in se enim elementa dum convertuntur, sicut in organo qualitatis sonus immutatur, et omnia suum sonum custodiunt.'

Augustine accepts the allegorical interpretation of the Bible, as Philo did. Indeed he admits that Ambrose's allegorical interpretations (themselves based on Philo) drew him to the Church (v. *Confessions* V, 14; VI, 4), and, before the assembled bishops at Hippo, it was Augustine in his turn who expounded the hidden meanings of the Bible and the Mysteries of Number.[7] As Peter Brown tells us in his biography of Augustine, for him:

> the Bible became a gigantic puzzle—like a vast inscription in unknown characters. It had all the elemental appeal of the riddle: of that most primitive form of triumph over the unknown which consists in finding the familiar hidden beneath an alien guise.[8]

Augustine could thus hold his audience spellbound when he explained why there were 13 apostles and yet only 12 thrones upon which they could sit (*Enarr.* 49, 9). By allegorical interpretation one could explore the spiritual, transcendent, world. The Bible was a test, a philosophical problem of Platonic dimensions and cast. One must rise above the 'letter' to the 'spirit'.[9] In this way the Bible was endowed with a range of meaning that made it literally encyclopaedic, both in its own content and in the range of learning that could be brought to bear upon it. It 'contained all knowledge useful to man, both sacred and profane. St Augustine accepted this Alexandrian concept and worked out its consequences for Christian education.'[10]

The overall strategy of the Christian Fathers of course differed from that of Philo, for they had to take the New Testament into account, if possible making the Old prefigure the New. (A typical example of this is the Pauline allegory of the crossing of the Red Sea, as baptism, in I *Corinthians* 10:1–16.) Their aim was to

25

'harmonize' the Old and New Testaments ('συμφωνειν', 'con-
cordare', 'consonare' were the words they used). Thus Milton, in
1645, in his 'Exposition upon the four chief places in Scripture,
which treats of Marriage, or Nullities in Marriage', entitles his
book *Tetrachordon*. The Bible was seen as a huge harmonic structure of verbal echoes. Brown summarizes the qualities of mind
displayed by Augustine in this type of exegesis:

> He is very much the product of a culture that admired a
> complete mastery of texts combined with great dialectical
> subtlety in interpretation. His memory, trained on
> classical texts, was phenomenally active. In one sermon,
> he could move through the whole Bible, from Paul to
> *Genesis* and back again, *via* the Psalms, piling half verse
> upon half verse. This method of exegesis, indeed, which
> involved creating a whole structure of verbal echoes,
> from every part of the Bible, was particularly well suited
> to teaching this hitherto quite unknown text, to an
> audience used to memorizing by ear. And, like a school-
> master, Augustine tended to present the Bible as a series
> of cruxes. He never relaxed for a moment the impression
> of a mind of terrifying acuteness.[11]

In all these traits Augustine was, as we shall see, immensely
influential, especially from the eleventh century on, when the
writings of Augustine, together with Chalcidius's *Timaeus* and
Boethius's *Consolation of Philosophy*, represented the most solid body
of theological and philosophical ideas available in Latin. These
texts kept Platonism alive in the Scholastic period before the new
translations from Greek and Arabic.

Augustine would thus have agreed with John Donne's principle
that:

> Nothing . . . seems so much to endanger the Scriptures,
> and to submit and render them obnoxious to censure and
> calumniation, as the apparence of Error in Chronology,
> or other limbs and numbers of Arithmetick: for, since
> Error is an approbation of false for true, or incertain for
> certain, the Author hath erred (and then the Author is
> not God) if any number be falsely delivered. . . .[12]

Thus in his chapter on the Ark in *Civitas Dei* XV, chapters 26 and

27, Augustine has to explain why the dimensions of the Ark are as they are, all this in accordance with his general principle that 'Noah's Ark signifies Christ and His Church in all things'. I shall quote from Augustine at some length, as this passage exemplifies quite clearly the principles of exegesis stated above.

> (The Ark) verily is a figure of God's city here upon earth, that is, his church which is saved by wood, that is by that whereupon Christ the mediator between God and Man was crucified. For the dimensions of the length and breadth of the ark do signify man's body, in which the Saviour was prophesied to come, and did so; for the length of man's body from head to foot is six times his breadth from side to side, and ten times his thickness measuring perpendicularly from back to front. Lay a man prone and measure him, and you shall find his length from head to foot to contain his breadth from side to side six times, and his height from the earth whereon he lies, ten times; whereupon the ark was made 300 cubits long, 50 broad, and 30 deep. And the door in the side was the wound that the soldiers' spears made in our Saviour. . . . And the ark being made of all square wood, signifies the unmoved constancy of the Saints; for cast a cube or square body which way you will, it will ever stand firm.

Augustine further admonishes us that these things are not 'written to no end . . . bare and insignificant actions', but are 'both true histories and mystical allegories, all concerning the prefiguration of the Church.'[13]

He also attempted numerological exegesis of the New Testament, for instance when he explains why the Apostles caught 153 fishes and drew them to land (*John* 21:11). He regards this as the total number of saints who will be resurrected. But he also sees 153 as the sum of the numbers from 1 to 17 (the seventeenth triangular number). Thus in the moral sense, 10 can denote the decalogue, and 7 the gifts of the Holy Ghost which make it possible for man to fulfil the 10 laws, thus becoming a saint. Augustine takes the fact that there were 7 disciples fishing as a corroboration of his exegesis.[14]

The *De Civitate Dei* itself is numerologically proportioned. It has

22 sections (perhaps symbolizing completeness, since 22 is the number of letters in the Hebrew alphabet). These comprise two groups of five devoted to refutation (the ten negative precepts of the Law), and three groups of four dealing with positive teachings (symbolizing the twelve apostles and the four Gospels).

In fact, the New Testament is remarkably lacking in the number system of the early (O.T.) tradition. As Hopper points out in his chapter on the early church writers, the Gospel of St John shows the nearest approach to deliberate number symbolism, in the triple appearance of Christ after death, and the dividing of garments into four parts (19:23). There is also the gathering of the elect from the four winds (*Matth.* 24:31) and the 153 fishes.

Other numbers perhaps not meant to be symbolic, yet certainly taken to be so in the Medieval and Renaissance periods, are Christ's appointment of seventy missionaries besides the twelve (*Luke* 10:1; cf. *Deut.* 10:20–22, and *Exodus* 24:1–4), and the forty days of Christ's temptation (in the tradition of the forty days of trial by flood, and the forty days of Elijah's solitude). Other favourite 'numerological' Biblical texts for exegesis were the vision of Ezekiel's Chariot and the Revelation of the Apocalypse of St John.

The number forty has a pleasantly complicated history. Its original significance apparently derives from the forty-day disappearance of the Babylonian Pleiades (Hesiod, *Works and Days*, I, 17), which coincided with the rainy season, an unpleasant period. Their return was a signal for the New Year Festival. These connotations seem to live on in the forty days of Lent, the forty years of Hebrew wandering in the desert (*Exod.* 16:35) and the forty-day period of isolation in Roman ports, which gives us our 'quarantine'; all of these end happily. In the Old Testament the main connotation of the number seems to be that of trial and privation. The Flood lasts forty days (*Gen.* 7:17); there were forty, or twice forty days of purification after childbirth (*Lev.* 12:2–5), and forty years of Philistine domination over Israel (*Judges* 13:1). Elijah's solitude and Christ's temptation correspond to these, as mentioned before, in lasting for forty days.[15]

As a third and final example of numerologically biased biblical exegesis, I should like to discuss Hugh of St Victor, who inherited the numerological tradition of allegorical exegesis and codified it.

He taught at the Abbey of St Victor in Paris from *c.* 1125 to his death in 1141. For Hugh and his school, to expound a text in its literal, allegorical, and tropological senses, was to teach a doctrine.[16] This doctrine was expounded by bringing to bear the highly formalized techniques of the *trivium* (used for the letter of the text), and the *quadrivium* (for its spirit). Thus in his *De Sacramento*, Hugh alludes to these seven 'university disciplines' when he tells us:

> A knowledge of words is considered in two ways: that is, in pronunciation and signification. Grammar pertains to pronunciation alone, dialectic pertains only to signification, and rhetoric pertains to both pronunciation and signification at once. A knowledge of things involves two considerations; that is, form and nature. Form appears in the external disposition of a thing; nature in its exterior quality. The form of a thing is considered either with reference to number, to which arithmetic pertains, or to proportion, to which music pertains, or to dimension, to which geometry pertains, or to motion, to which astronomy pertains. To the interior quality of things, however, physics is relevant.[17]

Hugh, it is at once apparent, has an extremely tidy, scholastic mind. His two discussions of the Ark on Augustinian lines are quite exhaustive, and actually include diagrams.[18]

In his *Exegetica*, ch. XV,[19] he attempted to codify the ways in which mystic numbers could be symbolically significant in the scriptures. He is not concerned so much with their static symbolic meanings, as with their symbolic computational properties. According to him they have nine of these. First, according to their position (*ordinem positionis*). Thus one, the first of all numbers, signifies the principle of all things, and two signifies sin, diverging from the 'primo bono'. Secondly, according to the quality of their composition (*qualitatem compositionis*)—two can be divided, thus signifying corruption and transitory things. Thirdly, according to the mode of extension (*modum porrectionis*). Thus eight after seven signifies eternity after mutability. (This is in accord with the doctrine of the eighth age after Judgment, when we shall be with God in eternity after our stay on earth, which was subject to the planetary 7-day week.) Nine within ten, signifies defect within perfection (a 'falling short'), eleven beyond ten, transgression of the measure (of the ten commandments). Fourthly, *secundum formam dispositionis*; thus ten, stretched out in a line, signifies the rectitude of faith, and a hundred expanded in breadth, the breadth of charity. Fifthly, according to the way the number is computed—thus ten is perfection, since it contains in itself all computations. Sixthly, according to multiplication—thus twelve signifies the universe, being a multiple of four (the corporeal) and three (the spiritual). Seventh, according to addition of its parts, thus six is perfect. Eighth, according to the (aggregate) number of its parts (*multitudinum partium*). Thus three signifies the trinity, four the four seasons of the year. Ninth and last, according to exaggeration. Hugh is here thinking of the occasions ('seventy times seven') when a number is used to suggest 'a great number of times'.

This typical logical ordering does in fact comprehend all the basic ways in which numbers are manipulated in order to have symbolic meanings. Taken together, they show that if one applied more than a few of Hugh's methods to a given number, it could be shown to have quite a large complex of symbolic meanings.

We can safely conclude that numerological exegesis as practised from Philo on, must have made some knowledge of number symbolism the possession of every educated Christian in those centuries, well up to the close of the Renaissance, in which an allegorical mode of understanding a literary text was intellectually respectable. It is this tradition, fostered by the Church Fathers, which will constitute the chief evidence to show that it is plausible to expect an occult number symbolism in Renaissance (and indeed Medieval) works of art.

I have not been able in this short account to do anything like justice to the very widespread character of numerological exegesis, for example to the tradition of interpretation of the Psalms fostered by Cassiodorus, which was designed amongst other things to show that the content of the psalms was appropriate to the numbers within the order supposedly given to them by the Seventy Elders. (Thus the fourth psalm was supposed to be spoken by the Church, which admonishes us to take the Gospel to the four corners of the earth.) My main aim in this section has been to show how the non-scientific, more purely symbolic and allegorical functions of numbers as originally described by Pythagoras were expanded within the Christian tradition. But during the early Christian era there were also Jewish and pagan thinkers who preserved the more abstract ideas of Plato concerning mathematics, especially as a 'synthesizer' of cosmological knowledge. We discuss these in the next section.

2 *Arithmology*

This second, parallel, numerological intellectual tradition is much more abstractly systematic and philosophical than that of Biblical exegesis, and yet the two traditions interacted quite strongly, as I hope will become clear in the sequel. This 'arithmological' tradition runs from Nicomachus of Gerasa (*c.* A.D. 100) through the encyclopaedists, Martianus Capella, in his *De Nuptiis Philologiae et Mercurii* (especially Book VII), Isidore's *Liber Numerorum*, and Rabanus, *De Numero*.

Their 'divine arithmetic' treats fairly systematically of the nature of particular integers, mostly within the decad: and of their corresponding deities, their moral attributes, and their function in cosmological thinking, the latter nearly always strictly derived from the *Timaeus*.

The Christian Platonists in this tradition were concerned to write a 'divine arithmetic of creation' in which the God of *Genesis* proceeds *more arithmetico*.[20] Their aim was avowedly theological, and their work, apart from allowing that number was involved with matter, provided no basis at all for any subsequent speculative scientific achievement, except in so far as it taught the elements of arithmetic. Indeed these metaphysical mathematicians must have held up scientific progress, for they were very little concerned with what actually and observably happens.

For them the ideal in knowledge was the deductive clarity and certainty of Euclid (as, in a very different way, it was for Descartes and Spinoza). Theological and arithmetical certainty were equated, and theological arithmetic was a kind of super-science of which actual practical arithmetic and geometry were mere shadows. For true mathematics leads to the immaterial and eternal. As Nicomachus puts it, divine number exists in the mind of the creating God:

> like some universal and exemplary plan, relying upon
> which as a design and archetypal example, the Creator of

the Universe gets in order his material creations and makes them attain their proper ends.

And later he says:

> All that has by nature with systematic method been arranged in the universe seems both in part and as a whole to have been determined and ordered in accordance with number, by the forethought and mind of him that created all things; for the pattern was fixed like a preliminary sketch, by the domination of number pre-existent in the mind of the world-creating God, number conceptual only and immaterial in every way, but at the same time the true and eternal essence, so that with reference to it, as to an artistic plan, should be created all these things, time, motion, the heavens, the stars, all sorts of revolutions. It must needs be, then, that scientific number, being set out in such things as these, should be harmoniously constituted in accordance with itself; not by any other but by itself.[21]

Nicomachus is perhaps the most interesting of all these writers. All Medieval arithmetics derive from his *Introduction*[22] which according to Robbins and Karpinski[23] is but a restatement of beliefs which were common property long before him, and is one of the *artes* or τεχναι, which were concise practical descriptions and systematic expositions of the principles of various arts and sciences. Nicomachus' *Introduction,* like Theon of Smyrna's *Expositio rerum mathematicorum ad legendem Platonem utilium,* is intended to explain the mathematical principles involved in the passages on the World Soul in the *Timaeus,* and the marriage number in the *Republic* (cf. *Intro.* II, 24, 6). It opens with a glorification of arithmetic, telling us that mathematical number merely prepares the student for divine number:

> For it is clear that these studies are like ladders and bridges that carry our minds from things apprehended by sense and opinion to those comprehended by the mind and understanding, and from those material, physical things, our foster brethren known to us from childhood, to the things with which we are unacquainted, foreign to our senses, but in their immateriality and eternity

more akin to our souls, and above all to the reason which is in our souls.[24]

Nicomachus goes on to explain number as the true and eternal essence, defines number, and classifies numbers as perfect, abundant, and deficient, distinguishing between types of evenness and oddness, and between prime numbers and relatively prime numbers (that is two numbers with no common divisor, and which will not divide into each other, for instance 21 and 25). He then tells us about figured numbers, and closes the book with a discussion of ten different types of ratios. Very importantly, he makes a distinction between quantities and numbers thus:

Numbers: absolute and per se = arithmetic
           in mutual relation = music
Quantity: at rest = geometry
        in motion = astronomy

These distinctions were to lie at the basis of the Medieval quadrivium (a term apparently first used by Boethius). We can see how, in bringing various spheres of knowledge to bear upon texts, Hugh of St Victor was almost inevitably mathematically biassed.

In order to do justice to the actual manner in which number symbolism of the arithmological type was explained, I should like to turn now to a particular text; the *De Nuptiis* of Martianus Capella (fl. A.D. 410–29). This is an encyclopaedic work which preserved for the Medieval period the ancient educational system of the seven liberal arts. It thus had very considerable influence, and is quoted by all the Renaissance authorities. In its seventh book (*De Arithmetica*) it provides in effect a summary of work in the tradition of Nicomachus, Theon, Porphyry, Boethius, Cassiodorus, and pseudo-Iamblichus.[25] My treatment follows Capella's own order of exposition.

He tells us that the monad is to be venerated as principle of all numbers which are procreated from it—indeed as father of all it could rightly be called 'Jove'. There is one god, one world, and one sun. Two makes a line and is called 'Juno'. It is feminine, also separation, and discord. Nevertheless it is 'capable of mediation' for it participates in both good and evil, and thus has something in common with justice, and it is mother of the elements, 'for from the number two the number four of the elements is produced; and it is the first Form of Parity (sc. Justice)'.

The number three is to be esteemed as perfect because it generates the perfect six and nine. It is the principle of odd numbers, and the first to have a beginning, middle, and end: 'thus it signifies the perfection of the world, for the monad is fitting to the creating god, the dyad to the generation of matter, and the triad, consequently, to the Ideal (sc. Platonic) Forms.'[26]

The perfection of the tetrad lies in its solidity. Furthermore, man has four ages, four vices, and four virtues. Five is the number of the world—or at least of its inhabitants, for the number is made of both sexes, three being male, and two being, as we have seen, female. Multiplied by odd numbers it perpetually repeats itself (*se semper ostendit*). Six is perfect for reasons we know of already, and is assigned to Venus. Seven is virgin, and Minerva. It is also Pallas, the moon goddess, for there are seven forms of the moon, and the numbers from one to seven added together make 28, the number of days of the moon's course. Seven is virgin because it is neither generated nor generating within the decad, that is, it is neither the product of numbers below ten, nor will it multiply with a number below ten to produce a number below ten, except of course unity, which was not considered a true number. One may well ask whether seven has anything to do with man. It has, for man has seven orifices in his head, 'sensibus praeparatos', two eyes, ears and nostrils, and one mouth. In the seventh month teeth appear, in the seventh year they change for new ones, and so on. Eight is the first cube ($2 \times 2 \times 2$) and is called Vulcan. It is perfect because it is covered by (*tegitur*) the perfect six, for a cube has six surfaces. Like the number two, the cube is the mother of all. This is asserted due to a confused etymological argument of Capella's—he is conflating the word for cube and the name of Cybele, the Great Mother (of Zeus, Hera, and other gods). Nine is perfect, and the more perfect, since it is made of the multiplication of the perfect triad by itself. It tends towards the end (that is, ten) and is thus called Mars (exactly why, it is difficult to imagine). Nine is the ultimate part of harmony (with eight it makes the tone, 8:9) and is also the number of the Muses. There are nine zones in the universe, that is the fixed sphere, the seven gods (*deorum septem*, i.e. the planets, astrologically considered) and the earth. The decad is of course above all other numbers, containing all their individual perfections. It is called Janus.

Having got the really philosophically important facts about

numbers out of the way, Capella goes on to tell us about simple arithmetic.[27] For instance he tells us what primes are, and other unsurprising facts, such as that odds added together will yield evens, but that even numbers will never yield odd. What is surprisingly illogical, is that in his mythological and arithmological excursus, Capella has used precisely those concepts which he only now gets around to defining in any properly mathematical sense. He goes on to retail simple arithmetic on a schoolboy level, explaining factorizability, perfect, abundant and deficient numbers, rectangular numbers, and so on. Then follows an elementary account of ratios, and what for us is the multiplication table.[28]

Capella's account is, to say the least, a rather bare and uninspiring one. I have passed on his information in almost as concentrated and breathless a form as it appears in his book. It is also rather elementary considered as operational arithmetic. Capella seems mainly to be concerned with numbers as Platonic forms, the supreme type of abstract universal with allegorical instantiation. Thus the number nine is a kind of locus of perfection—as the square of the divine triad, as the number of the muses, and as 'tending towards ten' (Hugh's 'modum porrectionis'). But for Hugh, as we saw, nine falls short of the perfect ten and is a defect within perfection rather than a striving towards it. We thus see how contradictory allegorical actions can be set up within the decad by successive commentators.

However, the Greeks, arithmologists like Nicomachus and Capella, and 'pure philosphers' like Plotinus[29] were mainly using mathematics to project what seemed to them to be a rational order for the universe in its creation and disposition. For the most part, they were deliberately using number symbolism in an allegorical way. That is, the assignation of Greek astrological deities to numbers, the symbolization of Justice by the number four, are essentially deviations in this tradition from an original more properly scientific cosmological cum astrological conception. But despite this original intention, in the Medieval period and beyond, the conception of allegorical levels of meaning allowed numbers to be given a wide variety of senses.

What emerges most clearly from these arithmologists is the concept of a creator mathematician, strictly in the style of Plato, yet adapted to varying religious views. Thus the monad—the originating principle of the number series, is formally identified with God (cf. *Nichomachus* VI, 8). For the monad, itself not a number, is an essence rather than a being (Plotinus, *Enneads* VI, 9, 3), and sometimes, like the decad, may be called a potential number, since the point, though not itself a plane figure, can originate plane figures (*Nichomachus* II, vi, 3). Thus as Originator the monad is both God, and good (*Enneads* VI, 9, 6; V, 1, 7).[30] According to Capella indeed, the monad is *all* that is good and desirable and essential. Macrobius takes this tradition to its extreme by identifying the monad with God or Mens:

> One is called monas, that is Unity . . . itself *not* a number, but the source and origin of numbers. This monad, the beginning and ending of all things, yet itself not knowing a beginning or ending, refers to the Supreme God, and separates our understanding of him (the One without number) from the number of things and powers following: you would not be so rash as to look for it in a sphere lower than God. It is also that Mind, sprung from the Supreme God, which, unaware of the changes of time, is always in one time, the present: and although the monad is itself not numbered, it nevertheless produces from itself, and contains within itself, innumerable patterns of created things.[31]

It is interesting to note in this context, that the Gnostic thinkers, principally centred in Alexandria, had a doctrine of emanations which according to Hopper 'is entirely germane to the generation of the decimal system by the monad'. This Gnostic belief was combated by the Church Fathers; indeed what we know of its doctrines comes largely from the way they are represented in these attacks. It was Manichaean in outlook; matter was evil; fate had seven demonic agents, keepers of the seven gates (these are perhaps the Babylonian planetary Gods).[32] As in Pythagoreanism, everything proceeded from the One, but the sensible world was not built by a geometrizing Demiurge but emanated out of the triadic harmony of Being, Life and Intellect in association with the four creative elements, or four elementary kingdoms. Irenaeus, in his refutation of the Gnostics (*Against Heresies* II, 24, 4) argues that their theology is fallacious, *not* because it is based on numbers, but because their scheme is incorrect! For they ignored the number five, everywhere manifest in the True Faith ('σωτηρ' and 'pater' have five letters, the Lord blessed five loaves, and fed five thousand people, there are five extremities of the Cross, five fingers, and five senses).

God as the One was brought into conjunction with the divine decad elsewhere in the more orthodox Christian tradition. For even the divine celestial orders are numerically controlled. There are nine orders of angels in whom the perfect three is reflected in itself (*super se reflexa*) (Bonaventure, *Sentences*, II, dist. 9, qu. 8, ad opps 2). Yet this perfection is secondary to the perfection of God—so the addition of the unity of the Godhead is necessary to complete the decad. (This is according to Capella's view of the number nine; compare the astronomical parallel of the counter-world which made up the celestial decad for the Pythagoreans.)

According to another school of thought, the original ten orders of angels were depleted by those who fell with Lucifer—and man was created to fill in the breach. The parable in Luke 15, 8–9, about the woman who loses one of her 10 silver coins and seeks diligently until she finds it again, was held to justify this view (Bonaventure, *Sentences*, II, dist. 9, qu. 7).

Even the doctrine of the Trinity may be of Neo-Pythagorean and Gnostic inspiration. According to Hopper:

> the paramount doctrinal weakness of Trinity, as the Arian heresy testifies, was the duality of the Godhead. The acceptance of Philo's 'logos', and its identification with the Son, was the first step towards a solution, but the addition of the third person, the Holy Ghost, provided indisputable evidence of unity. The presence of divine triads in all the Gnostic creeds was certainly a determining factor in the creation of the Trinity, but the underlying Pythagorean basis of contemporary philosophy necessitated the doctrine. That the Father and Son were One was questionable upon numerical as well as philosophical grounds. But Father, Son, and Holy Spirit, were unquestionably One by very virtue of being Three.[33]

He goes on to point out that many early writers, including Paul, seem never to have heard of the trinitarian doctrine. Thus the two New Testament references, one to a triad (*Matth.* 28, 19) and the other precisely to a Trinity (*John* 5, 7) are, particularly the latter, suspect as interpolations. References to the Trinity do not become common or definitive until the third century, and the doctrine did not receive final or official confirmation until the Council of Constantinople (A.D. 381).

The two traditions—exegetical and arithmological—which I have so far rather artificially kept apart, were of course combined by many thinkers. In the Renaissance, symbolic number was thought of as an inextricable mixture of the two. Thus numbers attracted clusters of often incompatible meanings, whose roots lay in both Christian and Pagan philosophical modes of thought. It may help the reader to give some examples of these 'clusters' of symbolic meaning, thus indicating that the repertoire of the numerologists was indeed a very large one.

For example, the dyad was regarded as evil not only on Biblical grounds because God failed to say on the second day of creation that He saw that it was good, and because the unclean animals entered the ark in twos, the clean ones in sevens, but also on more abstract philosophical grounds, of Gnostic-Manichaean parentage, because the dyad represents divisibility, a breaking away from unity (cf. Plotinus, *Enneads* V, 3, 4). Hence the dyad was the mother of matter or existence in those Manichaean schemes which regarded the created world as evil. This view went right back to Pythagoras.[34] According to Iamblichus in his *De Vita Pythagorae*, XXXVIII, he

> called the better of the opposed powers monad and light
> and right and unvarying and form and noble: the other,
> the worse power, dyad and dark and left, and varying
> and unstable and inconstant.

Two also came to represent any opposing entities, for instance mind and body, and thus represented man; for Plato all even numbers were of ill-omen.[35]

Hardly surprisingly, the triad had great prestige in the Christian era. Miss Smalley remarks that 'a Victorine was firmly per-suaded that all good things go in threes.'[36] According to Proclus, 'Every divine order has a unity of threefold origin from its highest its mean and its last term'.[37] Thus good Platonic reasons could be adduced for Christian doctrine. Porphyry and Iamblichus and Capella all repeat the doctrine that three is the first real number and is surface. It is also the first of the so-called marriage numbers. In Orphic cosmogony the marriage of Heaven and Earth is mediated by a third principle, Eros. In the Pythagorean tradition there are three stages of creation: (1) undifferentiated unity, (2) the separation into two opposite powers to create the world order and (3) the union of the opposites to generate life.[38] For Dante three symbolizes love.[39] For Capella, as we saw, the triad signified the perfection of the world.

The number seven is equally mixed in its meanings: I give it as an example because it shows the important strand of astrology in number symbolic thinking. It is as we know, Pallas the Virgin number. There are, furthermore, seven days of the planetary week (this convention was supposedly adopted in the first century B.C. in Alexandria) which were especially sanctified by the seven acts of creation in the now divinely ordained seven-day week of creation. There was also an astrological belief that the soul descends to earth through the seven planetary spheres, acquiring its virtues from the stars. After death it reascends, reaching at last the Eighth Heaven (i.e. the eighth sphere of the fixed stars) and enjoying eternal bliss. Dante's vision of the Church Triumphant occurs in the Eighth Heaven, and the apotheosis of the church militant is seen on the eighth step of Purgatory. Similarly at the end of *Troilus and Criseyde*, when Troilus has been slain by 'fierse Achille',

> His lighte goost ful blisfully is went
> Up to the holughnesse of the eighthe spere,
> In convers letying everich element;
> And ther he saugh, with ful avysement,
> The erratik styrres, herkenyng armonye
> With sownes ful of hevenyssh melodie.
>
> (Book V, 1807–13)

The number seven also has a good stock of Biblical meanings. For the Babylonians seven was the number of expiation and sacrifice, thus the clean animals enter the ark by sevens (*Genesis* 7; 2–3). For seven years Jacob served for Leah, and again for Rachel (*Genesis* 29). It is also the number of trial and punishment: for seven months the ark of the Covenant was in the land of the Philistines (I *Sam.* 6:1), and the Israelites were for seventy years in bondage (*Jeremiah* 25:11 and 29:10).

Thanne shewede he hym the litel erthe that here is,
At regard of the hevenes quantitie;
And after shewede he hym the nyne speres,
And after that the melodye herde he
That cometh of thilke speres thryes thre,
That welle is of musik and melodye
In this world here, and cause of armonye.

(Parliament of Fowles, 57–63)

Chaucer is describing here 'Tullyus of the Dream of Scipion', that is, the closing section of Cicero's *De re publica*, which he knew, with the commentary of Macrobius—who 'roghte not a lyte' of the contents of Chaucer's 'Olde book to-torn'.

Macrobius, whose 'world picture' Chaucer describes, flourished at the end of the fourth and beginning of the fifth centuries A.D. He was a polymath who attempted to epitomize and present in readily digestible form, like Capella, the matter of the seven classical arts, of grammar, rhetoric, dialectic, arithmetic, geometry, music and astronomy. According to Stahl[40] the *Dream of Scipio* was the 'most important source for Platonism in the latin West in the middle ages', which regarded Macrobius as an authority on Neo-Platonism (of which the real, that is the truly philosophical, authorities and originals are Plotinus, Porphyry, Iamblichus and Proclus).[41] About two thirds of Macrobius' commentary is digression—on Pythagorean arithmetic, on the harmony of the spheres, on astronomy, geography and the immortality of the soul. Large portions would serve as an adequate translation of the Greek pseudo-Iamblichus' *Theologumena Arithmetica*. The main theme of Macrobius is the origin and descent of souls (I, ix-xiv). I shall be concerned here with his Pythagorean numerology, and the influence on Macrobius of what he himself calls 'Plato's scroll and majestic discourse upon nature' (I, ii, 30).

In his fifth chapter, on numbers, Macrobius is concerned to show the numerical origin of material objects,[42] and to demonstrate the virtues of the individual numbers in the sacred decad. Like Plato he believes that mathematics 'draws the soul upwards'.

> this attribute of perfection is common to all numbers, for in the progress of our thought from our own plane to the Gods they represent the first example of perfect abstraction.

40

And numbers underlie creation. In this respect the number eight is especially important.

> That the number eight produces a solid body has been demonstrated above. But this number has a special right to be called full, for in addition to its producing solid bodies it is also without doubt related to the harmony of the spheres, since the revolving spheres are eight in number.[43]

Here again we have the essential ambiguity of this type of analogical thinking—does the number eight 'produce' solid bodies causally in the physical sense, or is Macrobius simply alluding to the fact that we can 'produce' a solid body on paper by joining eight points together, or is it a Platonic Form? In fact the latter must be intended, but there are definite overtones of both of the former. Secondly does 'related to' mean simply 'calls to mind' or is something causal intended here, too? One has to admit that here, as in so many places elsewhere, these writers' excited feeling of system led them to spot correspondences which were 'called to mind' rather than constitutive of the reality they were purporting to describe. One must also remember that their ideal of knowledge lay in knowledge of manuscripts, of their sources, whose wisdom they present and hand on; and that they often collate heterogeneous material. Hence the inevitable confusion and lack of a single core of meaning for many symbolic numbers.

Even so, men like Macrobius write in a truly poetic way, of a world in which everything is related to everything else, a world of occult relationships waiting to be discovered in metaphors, and preserved within an arcane tradition of philosophy. These correspondences, as opposed for instance to those of a Swedenborg, or more appositely, a non-numerically inspired Gnosticism, are embroidered upon the rigid structure of simple arithmetic. Thus one can make simple and intelligible moves within the system. The planes of thought—Biblical, properly Timaean cosmic harmonies, and astronomical numbers—correspond simply by virtue of the numbers they have in common. The range of thinking encompassed by numerology thus made it a fairly respectable candidate for a world view. Numbers were usable as the archsyncretizers of important knowledge.

I discuss Macrobius here, however, not because he is a typical hander on of number lore, but because he, with Chalcidius, passes on in relatively pure form the world scheme of the *Timaeus*. His extreme popularity in the Middle Ages allows us to say that in the *Somnium Scipionis* we have surveyed for us the Medieval 'world picture', in its larger aspects. Macrobius describes the constitution of the universe upon the model of the *Timaeus*, because it is Plato who has given the authoritative account of how things hang together, for 'we know according to Plato (that is according to the sanctuary of truth itself), that those bodies alone are closely held together which have a mean interposed between extremes to create a strong bond'.[44]

Thus he goes on to discuss the Platonic Lambda and the constitution of the World Soul, and the human soul, which according to Platonic precept is divided into three, reason, emotion and appetite.[45] 'Moreover all wise men admit that the soul was also derived from musical concords.'

The major re-emphasis which Macrobius gives to the Platonic account, and which was of great subsequent importance, lies in his account of the music of the spheres, the 'harmonia mundi', which could also be inferred from the Scriptures (*Job*, 38:7), 'cum me laudarent, simul astra matutina et jubilarent omnes filii dei'. He maintains that Pythagoras made his harmonic discoveries by using differently weighted blacksmith's hammers, and also by suspending the same weights on the stretched intestines of sheep or the sinews of oxen, which were then, presumably, plucked; and he then goes on to define the diapason, diatessaron, etc. Like Pythagoras, he generalizes this harmony. The musically ordered Platonic World Soul 'was to instill harmonious agreement in the whole world'.

> Thus the world soul, which stirred the body of the universe to the motion we now witness must have been interwoven with those numbers which produce musical harmony in order to make harmonious the sounds which it instilled by its own quickening impulse. It discovered the source of these sounds in the fabric of its composition.[46]

Macrobius also repeats some odd lore, which we will find cropping up in the Renaissance period, about the number seven. Here numbers are shown as having a quasi magical effect *in the physical world* if manipulated correctly. Thus, although he repeats the usual doctrine that seven is the Virgin, Pallas, in the decad (VI, 10, 11), since it is the only one which is a 'real' number and has no factors, and so on, he yet further confuses our associations for the number by quoting Hippocrates *On the Nature of the Child* (he is in fact following pseudo-Iamblichus). Hippocrates tells us that:

> the sperm expelled from the womb of a woman he had attended the seventh day had . . . a sack about it. For this woman who begged him to end her pregnancy, he prescribed vigorous jumping. He says that on the seventh day the seventh leap sufficed for expelling the seed with a sack such as we have described above.
>
> (VI, 64)

In this chapter I have tried to display two streams of numerological thinking which inspired Renaissance writers. The exegetical tradition became the property of all men who were well acquainted with their Bible. The arithmological stream of 'divine arithmetic' in the cosmological sense, is, as the reader will have sensed, uneasily poised in the Medieval period, between Christian and pagan. In the Renaissance we shall see that these two streams made up of Hebrew and pagan, are fully Christianized, and brought into close interaction.

The Medieval thinkers described above are still true in their fashion to their Greek beginnings—they rely on mathematics to help them do philosophy, even if their philosophy is simply handmaiden to their theology. In the absence of what we now call truly scientific and empirical thinking, they could still rely on Pythagoras to help them understand the harmonic structure of the Universe. What is new in this period is the literary emphasis given to numerology. Numbers are thought of in an entirely symbolic fashion, not as parts of an austere, truth-telling language, the language central to some of a culture's greatest intellectual advances, as mathematics was for the Greeks, but as a static structure upon which scraps of knowledge of all sorts could be hung. Allegorical modes of thought led Medieval men to think of numbers as existing on different levels, as indeed they thought of things in general. They possessed or prefigured quite different types of 'reality'. This is what I would call an inherent intellectual tendency to allegorize in search of understanding. This tendency carries with it great benefits in any attempt to unify disparate spheres of knowledge. But its attendant danger is that the bonds of unification will prove to be nothing but metaphor, and one may be left with a mere structure of words. The numerologists, by the philosophical standards they set themselves, won victory upon a purely verbal plane. But then they thought that these words were the Word of God. As long as God could be thought of as proceeding 'more geometrico' this was quite sufficient guarantee that numbers provided a map of reality, to be read in the Bible, in the arts of music and geometry, and in the heavens themselves in astronomical observation. If the stars moved at harmonic intervals, singing heavenly music to God as the angels did, so much the better. In the following two chapters we will find these ideas carried to their highest point of elaboration: after that they decline under the pressure of Biblical criticism and Newton's cosmology. But we shall see how, building on their Greek and Medieval legacy, Renaissance thinkers used numerology as a superbly subtle instrument for the unification of knowledge, and see later, how the literary qualities of the numerological systems at which I have hinted above were fully exploited in the arts.

Notes

[1] Philo, *De Opificio Mundi*, in *Philo* with an English translation by F. H. Colson and G. H. Whitaker, vol. I (London, 1929), p. 13f.
[2] *The Cambridge History of Later Greek and Early Medieval Philosophy* (1967), ch. VIII, pp. 137–8.
[3] Philo, *Leg. Alleg.*, II, 3; III, 148.
[4] Cf. *De Opificio Mundi*, 17, 20., *Specialibus Legibus*, I, 47–8.
[5] Op. cit., p. 156.
[6] XI, 30 (Dods trans. I, 475). The biblical tag is from *Wisdom* 11:21.
[7] Cf. *De Serm. Dom. in Monte* I, iv, 12 (Cited by P. Brown, *Augustine of Hippo* (London, 1967), p. 142).
[8] Op. cit., p. 253.
[9] On all these topics of allegorical interpretation, see esp. J. Pepin, *Mythe et Allégorie* (1958).
[10] Beryl Smalley, *The Study of the Bible in the Middle Ages* (Oxford, 1941), p. 13.
[11] Op. cit., p. 254, where references to Augustine are also given.
[12] *Essays in Divinity*, ed. E. M. Simpson (Oxford, 1952), p. 55.
[13] Tr. Healey, revised Tasker, Everyman edn., vol. II, pp. 93–4, 97.
[14] Cf. V. F. Hopper, *Medieval Number Symbolism* (New York, 1938), p. 80f., reporting *Contra Faustum* VI, Dods tr. V, 214–9.

Notes

15 I owe this set of examples to Hopper.

16 Hugh and his school are discussed in Smalley, op. cit., ch. III.

17 Cf. Migne, *Patrologia Latina*, 176, col. 185. I have quoted the translation given in Robertson, *A Preface to Chaucer* (Princeton, 1963), p. 297.

18 *De arca Noe morali* and *De arca Noe mystica*, *PL*, 176, cols. 617–9.

19 Migne, *PL*, 175, 22–3.

20 The Platonists in the school of Chartres maintained this tradition in their commentaries on the *Timaeus*, as is shown in this quotation from Thierry de Chartres: 'Quoniam . . . unitas (quae cunctorum est fons et origo) omnem numerum creat, numerus autem infinitus est, necesse est imitatem non habere finem suae potentiae. Unitas igitur est omnipotens in creatione numerorum. Sed creatio numerorum, verum est creatio. Unitas igitur omnipotens est in rerum creatione. At quod est omnipotens in rerum creatione illud unice et simpliciter omnipotens est. Unitas igitur omnipotens. Unitatem igitur deitatem esse necesse est.' *Tractatus* 36, ed. Haring, quoted in E. Garin, *Studi sul platonismo medievale* (Florence, 1958), p. 32.

21 *Introduction to Arithmetic*, tr. M. L. D'Ooge (University of Michigan Studies in the Human Sciences, vol. 16, 1926), Bk. I, iv, 2, p. 187, and I, vi, 1–2.

22 His words are almost literally reproduced in Capella (*De Nuptiis* VII), Boethius, Cassiodore, Isidore, Bede, Alcuin and Hugh of St Victor. Boethius' text proved to have the greatest subsequent influence.

23 *Studies in Greek Arithmetic* (1926), p. 16. (These studies are prefatory to the D'Ooge translation.)

24 Op. cit., Bk. I, iii, 6. D'Ooge, p. 186.

25 I quote and translate from the edition of Capella in the Teubner Library, ed. Dick, Leipzig (1925), 368–90.

26 Cf. op. cit., 369, 1, 9 ff.

27 Op. cit., 376 ff.

28 Op. cit., 381–5 and 389–90.

29 Cf. esp. *Enneads*, VI, 9.

30 According to Plotinus, God is also the 'sphaera intelligibilis', *Enneads*, II, 9, 14.

31 Macrobius, *In somnium Scipionis*, I, vi, 7–8, ed. W. H. Stahl (New York, 1952), pp. 100–1.

32 Quotation from Hopper, op. cit., p. 51. He describes the Valentinian gnosticism of the Pistis Sophia on pp. 57–9 of his book. The gnostic systems arose during the waning of the Roman official religion when the eastern mystery cults of the Egyptian Isis and Osiris and the Persian cult of Mithras were introduced into the Empire.

33 Op. cit., p. 73.

34 Cf. Diels, *Dox. Gr.*, p. 302. According to Dodds (*Pagan and Christian in an Age of Anxiety* (Cambridge, 1965), p. 14, the strongest later protagonist of this view was Numenius.

35 Cf. Plotinus, *Enneads*, VI, 6, 16, and Plato, *Laws*, V, 100.

36 Op. cit., p. 61.

37 *Elements of Theology*, L, 14, 8.

38 Cornford, *Plato's Cosmology* (1937), pp. 3, 4.

45

[39] Cf. Hopper, op. cit., pp. 163, 165, 175, 194.

[40] Op. cit., p. 10.

[41] On Macrobius' debt to Porphyry and Plotinus, see Stahl, op. cit., p. 32 ff. Quotation from Stahl, op. cit., p. 14.

[42] Cf. v, 12: 'Thus it becomes clear that numbers precede surfaces and lines (of which surfaces consist) and in fact come before all physical objects.'

[43] v, 4, and v, 15.

[44] vi, 23. Stahl, p. 104.

[45] vi, 45–7; vi, 42. Cf. Plato, *Republic*, IX, 580 D-E.

[46] II, i, 18–19; Stahl, pp. 192–3.

Three

Renaissance Thought

O comfortable allurement, O ravishing perswasion, to deale with a Science, whose Subject, is so Auncient, so pure, so excellent, so surmounting all creatures, so used of the Almighty and incomprehensible wisdome of the Creator, in the distinct creation of all creatures: in all their distinct partes, properties, natures, and vertues, by order, and most absolute number, brought, from *Nothing*, to the *Formalitie* of their being and state. By *Numbers* propertie therefore, of us, by all possible meanes (to the perfection of the Science) learned, we may both winde and draw ourselves into the inward and deepe search and vew, of all creatures distinct vertues, natures, properties, and *Formes*: And also farder, arise, clime, ascend, and mount up (with Speculative winges) in spirit, to behold in the Glas of Creation, the *Forme* of *Formes*, the *Exemplar Number* of all *thinges Numerable*: both visible and invisible, mortall and immortall, Corporall and Spirituall.

John Dee. Preface to *The Elements of Geometrie of the Most Ancient Philosopher Euclid of Megara.*[1]

John Dee, the Elizabethan astrologer-mathematician, here states a doctrine to which the previous chapters have accustomed us, yet with an entirely new fervour. This could be Marlowe's Faustus speaking. To repeat a commonplace about the Renaissance—the emphasis is now upon what men can *do* in their grasp upon the scheme of things, and to be drawn up into the 'inward and deepe search and vew' of things is to be both 'allured and ravished'. Such excitements are now the fruits of scholarship.

In our discussion of the pre-Renaissance period we have dealt with thinkers whose sources were relatively few (hence their interdependence) and whose strategy, for instance to reconcile the study of pagan classics with the teachings of orthodox Christianity, was often relatively simple. But in the Renaissance period one has to come to terms with the humanists' conscious programme of expansion of the study of classical texts. They did not disdain to study in detail and cite as undisputed authorities, authors whom we would now regard as minor, or to accept apocryphal works as authentic; though of course their chief literary reverence was still reserved for Homer, Cicero and Virgil, and their philosophical reverence for Plato and Aristotle. As is well known, a large part of this expansion was due to the translation of Greek texts into Latin—practically all of Greek poetry, historiography, and oratory was translated, and much of Greek patristic theology and of non-Aristotelian philosophy, and some few additional writings on science, mathematics and medicine.[2]

Thus all the texts so far discussed have a new status, as part of a new, immensely broadened stream of 'philosophical' literature. The attempt to reconcile texts, which all had the authority of antiquity, yet were written from so many different points of view, made Renaissance thinkers attempt to forge new bonds between disparate subjects and disciplines. The Medieval compartmentalization of knowledge such as we find in Capella, Hugh of St Victor, Macrobius and the greater Scholastic philosophers, dependent for its intellectual life upon the ability to make clear distinctions, is broken down. A thinker like Ficino conflates theology and philosophy, faith and knowledge, paganism and Christianity, by producing fine-drawn poetic analogies between them. The Medieval hierarchical order still retained all of its force, as did the principle of universal correspondence between things on different levels of being, and Renaissance thinkers used this framework in their attempts to understand the cosmos[3] as a whole. But they were not motivated by a single religious ideology, as was for example Plotinus. Their aim was rather to construct a system syncretically, and so to speak, euhemeristically, disregarding the conflicting premises upon which earlier thinkers had relied, and taking from them that which could be made to fit in with their overall strategy, which was, peculiarly enough, often that of constructing a 'genealogy of wisdom'. Reverence for antiquity thus led, paradoxically, to a totally ahistorical conflation of doctrines. (A first attempt to sort them out on a historical basis is found in Sir Thomas Stanley's *History of Philosophy*, London, 1656.) As a consequence, it is much more difficult to formulate what men like Ficino, or Bruno, personally believed, than it is to discover what Plato or Augustine or Plotinus believed—the main problem being that Renaissance thinkers try to hold doctrines from these thinkers, and many others, in some kind of uneasy combination. However, as we shall see, the numerological tradition manages to preserve a remarkable continuity in its tenets.

The 'root conflation' for the Christian thinkers was made, quite explicitly, between the Hebrew and Greek traditions, the Greeks of course including in an eminent position the later Nicomachus, Plotinus and Proclus. Thus Bongo in his *Numerorum Mysteria* (edition of 1618) says:

> Notum sane Numenii Philosophi verbum: Quid est Plato, nisi Moyses atticisans? . . . aut Plato Philonissat, aut Philon Platonissat, tanta est similitudo et ingenii, et dictionis cum Platonica.[4]

What is more, 'Eruditus erat Moyses in omni Aegyptorum sapientia.' We also find More in his *Conjectura Cabbalistica* (London, 1653) which is a mystical and moral interpretation of *Genesis*, saying (fol. B, 1):

> What is Plato but Moses Atticus? And for Pythagoras it is a thing incredible that he and his followers should make such a deal and doe with the mystery of Numbers, had he not been favoured with a sight of Moses his Creator of the world in six days and had the philosophick *Cabbala* thereof [not been] communicated to him, which consists mainly in numbers.[5]

The indebtedness of Plato to Moses was the prime ahistorical assumption made by Renaissance thinkers, who believed that it was possible to trace a single tradition, or 'prisca theologia' in all preceding thought. A second gross mis-assumption concerned the texts ascribed to the semi-mythical Egyptian priest, Hermes Trismegistus.[6] For the works which inspired the Renaissance Magus (and indeed most of our writers) and which were believed to be of profound antiquity, that is to be recording an ancient

49

Egyptian (Chaldean) wisdom not much later than the Hebrew prophets and patriarchs, and certainly much earlier than Plato (who was supposed to be influenced by them), were really written in the second and third centuries A.D. They were in fact Gnostic versions of Greek philosophy, 'the refuge of weary pagans seeking an answer to life's problems other than that offered by their contemporaries, the early Christians'.[7] These works were the so called *Corpus Hermeticum*, a collection of fifteen Hermetic dialogues. It is not known when they were collected, but they were known as such to Michael Psellus in the eleventh century. They are in fact by different unknown authors, who are always influenced by a cosmological framework of astrology. They do not form a system. Much astrological number symbolism was derived from this Hermetic literature. For Renaissance writers, Hermes Trismegistus was a real person, an Egyptian priest. Thus in the *Theologia Platonica* Ficino gives the Genealogy of wisdom as (1) Zoroaster, (2) Mercurius Trismegistus, (3) Orpheus, (4) Aglaophemus, (5) Pythagoras, (6) Plato.

The *Hermetica* were in fact dated in 1614 by Isaac Casaubon. The intellectual position of many 'philosophers' was thus destroyed: it was no longer possible to go back to a purer 'Egyptian' pre-Judaic and pre-Christian philosopher, nor possible to build a Hermetic natural theology. Seventeenth-century writers like Fludd and Kircher, however, both ardent numerologists, completely ignored Casaubon's discovery.

Thus for Ficino (1433–1499) the secret doctrine of Plato was refined by Iamblichus, Porphyry and Plotinus within a mysterious hermetic spiritual tradition of spiritual entities or 'essences', often mathematical ones. He ascribes to Plato esoteric truths of oriental origin, and appeals indiscriminately to Hermes Trismegistus, Proclus and pseudo-Dionysius to prove his points. For him Plato was essentially a religious mystic, and Platonism was a single doctrine revealed in varied sources. It is not surprising that, due to all this confusion, hardly a single doctrine we now associate with Plato was held by all Renaissance Platonists—doctrines such as those of the transcendental Forms, spiritual love, or the perfect political state.[8]

But, for our purposes, the most important, and fairly commonly held belief about Plato was this: that his *Timaeus* was a Pythagorean work. Thus Platonism was supposed to be at the centre of the Pythagorean and Hebraic systems that we have so far discussed. Ficino writes in a letter to Martin Uranio in 1489:

> Our Plato marvellously brought together the two ways
> (of religion and philosophy). Everywhere at once he is
> equally religious as well as philosophical, a subtle dispu-
> tant, a good priest, and fluent in speech. If you follow
> further the footsteps of the divine Plato, as you have
> begun to do, you will discover bliss in the judgment of
> God, and with God as your leader, you will attain to the
> same (judgment), especially as our Plato, together with
> the Pythagorean and Socratic doctrines, followed the
> law of Moses and prophesied the Christian law.[9]

It should not however be inferred from this that Pythagoras was not thought to merit independent attention: Heninger has documented this interest in his article 'Some Pythagorean Versions of the Tetrad'.[10] There he quotes Sir Thomas Elyot in his *Dictionary* (1538), describing Pythagoras as 'An excellent Phylosopher, whose Phylosophye was in mysticall sentences, and also in the Scyence of noumbers'; and Cudworth in his *The True Intellectual system of the Universe* (London, 1678) says, 'Pythagoras was most ancient of all the ancient Philosophers.' But even Pythagoras was supposed to be influenced by a 'prisca theologia'. Pico writes:

> It is written by Iamblichus that Pythagoras took the
> Orphic theology as a model after which he patterned
> and shapes his own philosophy. And for that reason
> alone are the sayings of Pythagoras called sacred, that
> they derive from the Orphic initiations, from which
> flowed, as from a fountainhead, the secret doctrine of
> numbers and whatever was great and sublime in Greek
> philosophy.[11]

Thus Renaissance numerological texts are woven of a number of different strands subordinated to a main purpose, and these strands are: ancient Orphic and Egyptian 'Chaldean' wisdom, the Hebrew tradition, with the Greek Pythagorean and Platonist traditions in attendance (the latter now brought up to full strength by translation), the Hermetica and the Cabbala, along with the Church Fathers, the Gnostics and the Neo-Platonists, especially Proclus and Plotinus.

A direct result of this syncretism is that numerological thinking becomes both immensely more sophisticated, and much more self-contradictory. There is a huge amount of repetition from text to text of the same ideas. It is impossible to indicate here everywhere that this has happened, for the price in sheer tedium of repetition is too high to pay. It should be assumed by the reader that most Renaissance authorities do have the greater part of the sources to play with, and do so, relentlessly. As Kristeller remarks, about the moral, educative, political and religious humanist treatises by such men as Petrarch, Salutati, Bruno, Valla, Poggio, Filelfo, Barbaro and Alberti, they

> are the works of consummate writers and scholars, but must appear somewhat amateurish to a reader acquainted with the works of the greater Greek, scholastic, or modern philosophers. They often seem to lack not only originality but also coherence, method and substance, and if we try to sum up their arguments and conclusions leaving aside citations, examples and commonplaces, literary ornaments and digressions, we are frequently left with nearly empty hands.[12]

It can thus be assumed by the reader that the writers discussed in this chapter are all acquainted (though of course to varying degrees) with all the material discussed in the preceding chapters. Renaissance thinkers were trying to transform old systems of thought. They did not attempt to produce original systematic philosophy, in the sense we accept, with Locke, Spinoza, Kant and Wittgenstein (in the *Tractatus*) before us. What I have tried to do is to show how different selected thinkers adapt the stock of number symbolic thinking to an overall intellectual strategy— magical, astrological, biblical, exegetical, to the explanation of Biblical Creation, the extension of the Pythagorean concept of world harmony, scientific cosmology, and so on.

Attempts to trace with any exactitude the features of numerological Pythagoreanism and Platonism are further complicated by the Renaissance liking for the occult. For it is extremely important to remember (especially when we look for evidence of numerological influence on works of art), that the Pythagorean doctrines were secret ones. Bongo, for example, says that we have to be careful in our dissemination of the divine and rational knowledge of number, 'nec margaritas mitti ante porcas' ('not casting pearls before swine') (Praefatio, p. 2), and continues 'occulta enim non debant communicari omnibus' ('occult things are not to be communicated to everyone'). One strong reason for this attitude lay in the fact that numerology gave the hidden clue to the structure of the whole of creation. For the basic assumption of Renaissance Neo-Pythagorean thought is still the axiom derived from Solomon, and confirmed by Plato, that 'omnia in mesura et numera et pondere disposuisti'. The universe was numerically ordered. 'Nam mundus uterque Numeris est dispositus' says Bongo (p. 2), and Agrippa believes that 'proportion of numbers' was 'the principall pattern in the mind of the Creator' (II, ii, 170). Even the astronomer Kepler believed that God is 'geometricae fons ipsissimus, et, ut Plato scripsit, aeternam exercens *Geometriam*'.[13] Whether the universe was thought of as 'designed' in the Timaean tradition, or 'begotten' or 'emanated' in the Gnostic one, or whether God be a mythical Demiurge or Metaphysical first Cause, it had always been thought of as having a numerological design, or plan. As John Donne tells us: 'God himself made all he made according to a pattern, God had deposited and laid up in himself certain forms, patterns, Ideas of everything that he made. He made nothing of which he had not preconceived the form.'[14]

It is a great motive of Renaissance speculation to ascend to the First Cause and contemplate this plan. We shall see it later as the primary inspiration behind Kepler's attempts to explain the astronomical order. As Cardinal Nicholas of Cusa, whose writings inspired a great deal of Renaissance numerological thought, said:

> Mathematics are of a very great help in the Understanding of different divine truths. All our greatest philosophers and theologians unanimously assent that the visible universe is a faithful reflection of the invisible, and that from creatures we can rise to a knowledge of the Creator, 'in a mirror and in a dark manner', as it were. The fundamental reason for the use of symbolism in the study of spiritual things, which in themselves are beyond our reach, has already been given. Though we neither perceive it nor understand it, we know for a fact that all things stand in some relation to another: that, in virtue of this relation, all the individuals con-

stitute one universe and that in the one Absolute the multiplicity of beings is unity itself. Every image is an approximate reproduction of the exemplar: yet apart from the absolute Image or the Exemplar itself in unity of nature, no image will so faithfully or precisely reproduce the exemplar as to rule out the possibility of an infinity of more faithful and precise images, as we have already made clear.[15]

All these thinkers had this great ideal, which comes to them undiluted through Greek and Medieval thought: the ideal of Order, the desire to anatomize the world's body, in order to show how all its parts correspond and work together. The ideas of hierarchy, universal analogy, correspondences between spiritual orders of being, of universal correspondences between all created things, are all principles and axioms in this search for order.

There is an extra difficulty in following the strangeness of some of the thought processes involved in making these 'geometrizing' explanations. In the case of Pythagoras and Plato, whether one believes they constructed a myth, or that they wrote theology, one can see their works as attempts to understand the cosmos with the equipment available. But as soon as we can feel the tension in the Renaissance between the Platonic Neo-Pythagorean way of thinking, and that of observation and experience (for instance that of a Tycho Brahe, a Bacon or a Galileo), it becomes difficult to see what the advantages were of sticking to what seems to us an archaic way of thinking. The motives seem to be partly religious and aesthetic ones, which we can sympathize with, and partly a wilful obscurantism and mysticism (for example in the works of Robert Fludd).

Certainly at issue is the Renaissance idea of the dignity of man.[16] For Pico, man's worth lay in his ability to be familiar with different levels of being. He can contemplate the orders of angels or the lower levels of existence (the mutable sub-lunary world) at will. He also, according to Pico, rests secure in his knowledge of his place in the hierarchy. All the writers to be discussed in this chapter would agree with him. To understand them properly we must be able to imagine their triple world scheme.

This is a hierarchy of three worlds, genuinely believed to exist. They correspond to a philosophical distinction, clear to Plato and the Neo-Platonists, about the sorts of things we can think about, and the ways in which we can think about them. They are the world of the senses 'here below'; the intelligible world (the kind which seems to be both free and not free of sense experience, for example mathematical); and the super-sensible world (of the One, and of God and his angels). As we shall see, these three worlds receive different sorts of characterizations. But when we find Pietro Bongo talking about the ultra mundane world of God, and angels, the celestial world of the heavenly bodies of astrology, and the mutable sublunary world here below, we must remember that it seemed to Renaissance thinkers that there *had* to be such orders of being, and, what is more, that man's chief dignity and wisdom consisted in his ability to think about them, and especially in his ability to seek and explain their relevance to each other. This is why the science of astrology was taken so seriously. It was not simply a system of code signs for reading off the course of a man's life for merely practical purposes; it was the science which demonstrated the relationship between fundamental orders of being.

Man can range, intellectually, through these orders of being; he even contains them in himself microcosmically, and corresponds to them. Thus Giorgio, whom I discuss in the following section, speaks of Christ as 'Le Grand Homme Archétype' who, because he is perfect, contains in himself 'toutes les choses inférieures', and we shall also see Agrippa assert that man 'doth contain and maintain in himself all numbers, measures, weights, motions, Elements and all other things which are of his composition. . . .' Further, George Herbert in his *Man*, a poem which can only be understood in the light of the numerological tradition, says:

> Man is all symmetrie,
> Full of proportions, one limbe to another,
> And all to all the world besides;
> Each part may call the farthest brother,
> For head with foot hath private amitie,
> And both with moons and tides.
>
> Nothing hath got so farre
> But Man hath got and kept it as his prey;
> His eyes dismount the highest starre;

He is in little all the sphere:
Herbs gladly cure our flesh, because that they
Finde their acquaintance there.

I hope that the accounts given below, of four types of Renaissance numerological thinking, will persuade the reader that Herbert meant these lines quite literally.

Giorgio's *Harmonia Mundi* (1525) translated as *L'harmonie du Monde* (1579) by Guy le Fevre de la Boderie, is an elaborate Christianized version of the Platonic order of creation in the *Timaeus*. The work itself is designed to echo the structure of creation; as Guy says, introducing the work in his 'Epistre à Monsieur des Pres':

> Donc nostre autheur imitant au plus pres qu'il a peu l'ordre du monde, ancois l'Ouvrier & Architecte d'iceluy, a premierement divisé & comparty ceste harmonie du monde en trois Cantiques, chasque Cantique en 8 Tons ou Livres, & Chasque Ton en plusieurs chapitres, si bien conioincts et alliez, et si cointement distinguez et ordonez tous ensemble: que la Methode et clarté, voire le mesme ordre du monde univers, s'y decouvre et reluyt manifestement.

Giorgio attempts to bring the whole of theological, cosmological and Biblical knowledge within the single 'discipline' of the language of music.[17] By using the metaphors of 'consonance' and 'accord', and by linking these disparate universes of discourse by the bonds of the numbers they mention, he produces a unified system, whose main aim is to show how beautiful and proportioned and harmonious everything is. Numerology is used strategically as a kind of super discipline to unify all the others. It provides a key for the polymath: it also puts all that Giorgio wishes to tell us into an essentially aesthetic order. He is not only 'doing philosophy', he is also producing a work of art whose order mirrors for us the order of creation. In admiring the one we perforce admire the other. And Giorgio as an artist aspires to be as a god in the creation of his own work—'infinite in faculty'.

In the first Canto Giorgio justifies God as the one Creator, claims truth for the Catholic tradition of theodicy, gives a quite strictly Platonic account of Creation, explaining the building and distribution of the elements 'par les nombres quaternaires' (canto I, ton. 3, ch. 13), describes the orders of angels, and the consonance on earth of elements with the planets, and then goes on to retail the doctrine of the proportions of man as microcosm. He then maintains that the proportions of the Ark reproduce those of a man in height, width and depth (300:50:30). His aim in this Canto is to show how everything in the angelic, celestial and elementary worlds is in numerical consonance with everything else, usually in triadic patterns.

The second Canto is about Christ, showing Him as containing all things, so that 'toute Harmonie procede du Verbe', and Christ is 'le grand Home Archetype coprenant de faict en soimesme toutes les choses inferieures'. A numerical correspondence worked out in detail here is that between the twelve signs of the Zodiac, the twelve tribes of Israel, and the twelve Apostles (canto II, ton. 7, ch. 12).

This association of the Christian with the astrological looks suspiciously unorthodox—so Giorgio takes great care to assert human free will, even though the stars are the Hermetic 'Governors' through which God rules the world. He tries in accord with this to make a distinction between the human, and the machine of the universe. He thus projects a whole universe allegorically, subdued to an arithmological order by God, in which everything is in literal harmony with everything else. Thus there is a 'Harmonie des Cieux tant pour la distance, que pour la consonance des mouvements' (canto I, ton. 8, ch. 16)—all Antiquity has attested this. (He cites Censorinus, Pliny, Eratosthenes, and Pythagoras.) Upon a purely theoretical plane, he works out those proportions which were to intrigue genuine astronomers: 'Depuis la terre iusques a la Lune, il y a cent et vingt et six mille stades, et sont l'intervalle d'un ton.' Thus, echoing Macrobius before him, he concludes that 'toute la machine du Ciel est comme un instrument harmonique distingué des distances sonoreuses, et lié de nombres accordés'.

The third Canto is concerned with the harmony between and within the soul and the body, showing how harmony between Intelligence and the Heavens gives power over all things. But the Holy Ghost alone can harmonize the tetrachord of the humours and the passions, reconciling the order in man with the 'Grand et divin tetraktys'. The tetraktys is as much a theme throughout this Canto as the triad was in the first.

The sources of Giorgio's thinking are the expected Neo-Platonic, Hermetic and Cabbalistic ideas. Guy le Fevre admits that he and his author have 'pillé' other authorities for 'leur plus belles plumes . . . leur plus chers Ioiyaux'. Though Moses and the Prophets are allowed precedence over the pagans, the whole of canto I, ton. 2, is given over to discussion of the authority of the sages. They disagree, and the Catholic doctors agree, but apparently discordant ancient authorities *can* be reconciled, since they speak in enigmas anyway, especially when performing before 'un peuple rude et grossière'. For Giorgio, the fact that the Platonists had an 'entendement divin' and the Catholics were 'enseignez de l'esprit saint', comes to the same thing. And in any case, 'innombrables Hebrieux, Chaldees, Grecs et Latins [following Plato and Moses] ont remply le Monde de livres tous sonnans d'un mesme accord'. Besides, Plato and Pythagoras may well have had their knowledge from the prophets or their auditors.

These considerations lead to the following defence of allegories and enigmas in the Introduction. It is important, since it indicates the way Giorgio's own work is to be understood. For we are told here that it is allegorization that reduces diverse sources to a single message: for the account of the building of the Ark, and of the tabernacle and temple of Solomon, Ezekiel's vision, and the Apocalypse:

> ne chantent qu'une mesme chanson, bien que diversement, comme fort bien entendent ceux qui scavent Pythagorifer et Philosopher par la Mathematique, qui comme elle soit trenchée d'un quarrefourc, nous monstre pour expliquer les choses naturelles et divines quatre voyes et grand chemins [i.e. of allegory] tous issans de l'Unité et de ses nombres. . . .

Just after the passage quoted here Giorgio goes on, like Hugh of St Victor, to attach a specific type of mathematics to different intellectual disciplines, which also provide four approaches to understanding; number (arithmetic proper), measuring (geometry), music (harmony), and celestial arithmetic (astronomy). The reasoning here is complex.

Le Fevre believes that all number comes from the number four (the quarrefourc) which 'contains' the decad, hence all numbers. He would hold that the modes of understanding are all contained in the four senses of allegory (literal, allegorical, tropological, and anagogical).[18] He also knows that the university disciplines of the quadrivium are four. But he gives numerology precedence, saying that our understanding of divine and natural things all really comes from number. He says this because he believes that only a numerological key can unlock the secrets of divine writings such as those describing the building of the Ark, the tabernacle and temple of Solomon, as well as the Apocalypse and Ezekiel.

To prepare us to be able to do this, the Introduction then provides us with a quite conventional account of number symbolism as we have so far encountered it: two is matter, the mother of number, the quaternary is a symbol of the four elements and contains all musical harmonies, all multiples of ten return to unity, and so on. This is followed by an account of perfect and abundant numbers, of the general significance of the major astronomical numbers, and the nine heavens and orders of angels, of the seven planets, 'instruments autants d'influence et de vertu, qui iouxte les sept mesures surmondaines du S. Esprit . . .' (this despite being within the decad 'vierge et pucelle'), and the twelve signs of the Zodiac, presided over by twelve angels, which are twelve 'portes et signes du ciel' corresponding to the twelve gates of Jerusalem in the Apocalypse.

Thus we are primed to see the controlling framework of what follows as one of numerical correspondences between things. Indeed Giorgio in his preface to the first Canto tells us that knowledge of number is necessary if we are to understand *anything*:

> Les arts semblablement, le nombre osté, s'évanouissent du tout: et ce qui est le principal, il asseure que le nombre est bien cause de tous biens, mais non pas d'aucun mal. D'ou vient que celuy qui veut etre heureux, et qui desire de sonder et rechercher les choses célestes et divines, ne doit point ignorer le nombre.

These are, of course, not merchants' numbers. Nor are we concerned with historical influences of texts, the history of a doctrine, or a reconciliation of canonical dogmas, that is, a straightforward account of Christian belief. Giorgio's thinking is entirely ahistorical. His main aim is to spot influences, or 'harmonies' or 'consonances' in the widest metaphorical sense. In this way, not surprisingly, apparently conflicting beliefs can be reconciled ('harmonized'). This can be done in any case in which numbers (especially in a Biblical passage), or zodiacal signs, or the Platonic proportions can be made to coincide. These numerical coincidences are taken to show that all these apparently heterogeneous bits of knowledge really fall within one single structure:—that expounded by the *Harmonia Mundi*! God, his creation (Platonic and Mosaic), the Old and New Testaments, Christ, astronomy and astrology, the soul and its harmony, the elements, the nine orders of angels, the microcosm of man, are all bound together by these numerical correspondences, spawned out of the monad, the triad, the quaternary, the twelve signs of the zodiac and the Platonic Lambda.

God is approached upwards through his creation for: 'il nous est permis de monter aux choses divines . . . procedant de ces choses visibles ou invisibles de Dieu par une Harmonique alliance qu'elles ont entre elles fort sonoreuse et bien accordées'.[19]

In the first Canto the author ascends to God the Supreme monad by relentlessly pursuing patterns of three and four—the quaternary is 'le racine et commencement de tous nombres', 'car l'assemblement depuis l'unité jusques au quaternaire produit la disaine'. The four elements are thus allied to the three times three spheres by 'la charme et ensuite des causes, montant . . . premierement par les quatres eschelons de l'eschelle de nature'.

God's creation took six days (canto I, ton. 2, ch. 11), because six is the marriage number called 'Gamon ou le nociers d'autant que ses parties mises à coté de luy l'engendrent', and 'le six premier nombre parfait convient à Dieu le souverain Ouvrier ou à sa fabrique, à laquelle rien ne deffaut'. It is also a perfect diapason (presumably by addition, four plus two). He thus even has a chapter to show how 'toutes choses sortent de Dieu par le nombre six' (canto I, ton. 8, ch. 8).

Giorgio elaborates his vast musical metaphor through over seven hundred pages (of the French translation). He pursues every possible analogy. But his book eventually has the role of a dictionary, not that of a building or organic body. Admittedly in Canto I, ton. 5, he explains the Platonic Lambda and explains in relatively orthodox fashion how musical geometrical and arithmetical proportions govern the way in which the soul and the whole world is constructed (ch. 11). But this is pretty well the limit of his attempts to use numbers in a structural sense: 'Donques cette Machine du Monde consiste du nombre simple, quarré, et cube conduit en souveraine consonance.'

Although we are promised a unified system then, we do not get it. As we have already seen, numbers used symbolically had come by now to have so many meanings that any exhaustively systematic use of them is quite impossible. Pythagoras' musical and Plato's cosmological uses are really the first and only ones which have any proper consistency and logic. Biblical exegesis and astrology and musical proportions on the other hand will not mix. They are bound to clash—astrology and Christianity are in any case in doctrinal opposition (though it is ironic to reflect that the Old Testament does in fact contain the vestiges of Babylonian astrological symbolism). Actually Giorgio is much concerned to keep it under orthodox Christian control: we are asked to admire the orderly machine of the universe, not to try to influence its operation. Everything is kept within the anodyne terms of the musical metaphor he is exploiting. So he tells us that 'L'eau resonne avec Mercure et Saturne' (canto I, ton. 4, ch. 15) and 'Quelles choses harmonisent avec Jupiter' but little more. Milton is, incidentally, indebted to this way of thinking when he writes in *Il Penseroso* of:

> . . . those daemons that are found
> In fire, air, flood, or underground,
> Whose power hath a true consent
> With planet or with element.

For he uses the word 'consent' which contains the meaning of the Latin 'concentus', harmony, or consonance.

Contrasted with the attempts made by men like Giorgio to describe creation by using a literary form supposed to mirror the ideas in the mind of creating God—i.e. whose 'plan' is on an anagogical level the 'plan' for the whole universe—are the chronological or quasi-chronological accounts of men like Du Bartas in his *Sepmaine* and Pico in his *Heptaplus*. These are, essentially, commentaries on *Genesis*, and are more specifically tied to the Christian tradition, yet they incorporate traditional Neo-Pythagorean elements. This free—ranging interpretation was regarded as perfectly licit (as part of the tradition of allegorical exegesis of the Bible). For as Bongo points out, the succession of days in the Genesis account of creation is given only for our human understanding: creation was really instantaneous. 'Credibile est utique Deum in agendo nequaquam tempus exquirere.'

The Huguenot Du Bartas (1544–90), according to C. S. Lewis,[20] came nearest to making poetry in the later metaphysical style we associate with Donne. His *Sepmaine* (the seven days of creation, 1578), and *Second Sepmaine*[21] (an unfinished account of early events in the world's history, 1584) had a huge influence, not least upon Milton, and the former was, in its translation by Joshua Sylvester, doubtless 'Sunday reading' in many protestant homes. Not only does it provide an easily digestible account of Biblical events adorned by many up to date similes (all carefully 'signalled' to the reader in the margin), but it also contains, encyclopaedically, much useful information, needful for the construction of a truly Protestant world view. For instance, it attacks judicial astrology (p. 4), it confutes the opinion of Copernicus (pp. 32–3), explains the Zodiac and principal stars (p. 33f.), says that a complete revolution of the firmament takes seven thousand years (p. 34; conceding on the way that celestial bodies do affect non-celestial ones, for accidents succeed eclipses (p. 35)), and in the section with which we shall be most concerned (the fourth part of the second day of the second week, 'The Columes') it gives an account of the liberal sciences. Like so many writers of the period, Du Bartas has views upon the 'genealogy of wisdom'. He believes that Egyptian knowledge predates the Greek:

> The Memphian priests were deep Philosophers,
> And curious gazers on the sacred Stars
> Searchers of Nature, and great Mathematicks;
> Yet any letter knew the ancient'st Atticks.

Hebrew is a principal tongue because of its numerical properties.[22]

Du Bartas' work is significant for us because it presents basic number lore in easily digestible and less mysterious form; and the fact that this lore must have been widely accepted via Du Bartas constitutes strong evidence that the world views described in this chapter were not entirely arcane, and were accepted and understood by most literate persons. He treats of the themes we have come to expect: of Creation by God,[23] of the events of the Old Testament, and of astronomy and astrology. He gives an exposition of the bare outline of what underlies more systematic writers like Giorgio: he treats simply of harmonic proportions, and he gives a very straightforward account of the dead. This is so simple that we may suspect it to be allusive, and to have needed some 'filling in' by the reader.

Thus he imagines Arithmetick as 'stately deck'd in most rich Attire;/All kind of Coins in glistening heaps lie by-her . . . Down by her girdle hanges a Table-book/Wherein the chief of her rare Rules are writ,/To be safeguarded from times greedy bit' (136). And her numbers are; One: 'the right/Root of all Number; and of Infinite';

> Loves happiness, the praise of Harmony, . . .
> No number, but more than a Number yet,
> Potentially in all, and all in it.

Two is 'first number, and the Parent/Of female pains', and is surprisingly not called evil by Du Bartas, who in an account of Creation ought not to have missed this trick.
Three is:

> The eldest of odds, Gods Number properly. . . .
> Heaven's dearest number, whose inclosed Center
> Doth equally from both extremes extend,
> The first that hath a beginning, midst and end.

Four is: 'Number of Gods great Name, Seasons, Complexions/Winds, Elements, and Cardinall Perfections.'[24] Five is Hermaphrodite: 'never multiplied/By't selfe, of Odd, but there is still discri'd/His proper face'. Six is perfect, of course, and seven is 'Criticall and double-sexed' (it contains three and four). Eight is merely the 'double-square', nine is the number of the Muses, and ten 'doth all Numbers force combine'.

Du Bartas thus does his duty rather skimpily, by the encyclopaedic tradition of Boethius, Capella and Macrobius. As Simon Goulart puts it in his Commentary:

> In forty verses or thereabouts, the Poet comprehendeth
> the principall grounds of the infinite secrets of Arith-
> metike, who list to examine that which the Ancients and

Moderns have written, should find matter enough for a large book.[25]

Du Bartas goes on to tell us about geometry:

> The Crafts-man's guide, Mother of *Symmetry*
> The life of Instruments of rare effect,
> Law of that Law that did the World erect,

thus reminding us that, even for a Huguenot protestant, God geometrizes constantly. There is in fact a remarkable lack of close reference to the *Timaeus* in Du Bartas; for instance he tells us that the elements are in proportion (10–11 and 17), but does not elaborate upon the mathematical means by which this was achieved. He then goes on to give an account of astronomy, explaining its technical terms (139–40) and concludes with a description and praise of Music in terms that are by now familiar to us. Music is that

> . . . sacred harmony
> And Numb'ry Law, which did accompany
> The Almighty-most, when first his Ordinance
> Appointed Earth to rest, and Heaven to dance.

And he describes the harmony of the spheres whose

> Rare Quier with th' Angels Quier accord
> To ring about the praises of the Lord,
> His Royall Chappell, richly beautified
> With glist'ning Tapers and all sacred Pride. (141)

It was the power of these two celestial worlds, of the stars and the angels (or devils) that the Renaissance magi tried to exploit. They tried to manipulate the natural sympathies in things, and through the arrangement and correct use of 'lower' things to draw to their level the powers of 'higher' things. Thus, most typically, the magus found occult stellar virtues in natural objects.

The magus or magician was a kind of heroic figure in the Renaissance (as the Faust legend testifies). Magic for him was a kind of 'prototype of scientific knowledge', in Mazzeo's phrase.[26] He had a secret knowledge of the hidden properties of things which gave him power over nature. This interest attracted men of the intellectual stature of Ficino, Pico, and Bruno. One must not

think, then, of the Renaissance magus as a kind of wizard of the
fairy tales. His quest was for understanding; for an ultimate
transformation of himself as knower. Granted his triple world
view, he sought influences between these worlds which were for
him of a genuinely sacred nature. As Walker remarks, 'Magic
was always on the point of turning into art, science, practical
psychology, or above all religion'.[27] There was, of course, some
tension between orthodox Christianity and magic. Men like
Giorgio and La Boderie tried to reconcile the two. But Agrippa
and Paracelsus were more attracted by the overtly demonic; by
invoking angels, demons, planetary influences, and by using
talismans, secret signs, ritual and emanations; and they make
little attempt to make their doctrines part of the Christian
framework.

Marlowe's Faustus thus says:

> Divinitie Adieu,
> Those Metaphysickes of Magicians,
> And Negromantike bookes are heavenly:
> Lines, circles, sceanes, letters and characters:
> I, these are those that Faustus most desires.

He explicitly abjures divine study and takes to Black magic. He
knows that knowledge of astrology, and of languages, especially
the Hebrew of the Cabbala, and of the sympathies between the
physical elements, gives him power:

> He that is grounded in Astrologie,
> Inricht with tongues, well seene in minerals,
> Hath all the principles magic doth require.

And by arrangement of the right signs and elements within a
circle he can conjure up the devil himself:

> Within this circle is *Iehouahs* name,
> Forward and backward anagrammatiz'd
> The breviated names of holy Saints,
> Figures of euery adiunct to the heavens,
> By which the spirits are enforst to rise. . . .[28]

Thus the aim of the magus practising 'white' or good magic (like
Prospero) was to call down upon earth good planetary or celestial
influences; of the 'black' magician, to raise up demonic forces.

The active agents for this calling down (or up) were two—psychological and physical. The *vis imaginativa* of the magus co-operated with a proper configuration of earthly objects. These objects were, as Walker tells us[29] basically of four types, and within each of the four there is an accepted occult force and also a suspect one. The first is the *vis imaginum*, which harnesses the forces of meaning and beauty in the visual arts, and more suspectly, of occult figures and characters (talismans, planetary signs), and the second type is the *vis verborum* which could be used licitly in poetry or oratory, but also as incantation, in which words were thought of rather in the way primitives think of them, as having power over the essence of the things they name. The third type of magic is the one we are concerned with. It is the *vis musices*—again, quite conventionally acting through the imagination in music and song, but acting with occult force as we shall see, via the proportions and numbers underlying music, which were thought to harness planetary forces through a correspondence with the harmony of the spheres. The fourth type is the *vis rerum* in which things are thought of as having elemental (sc. physico-chemical) properties, but also as having occult qualities of correspondence with the celestial order, such as we saw mentioned by Giorgio. The operation of all these types of magic had effect via the *vis imaginitiva*, upon both the magic worker, and upon others. Magic could thus be used by different men to very different ends. For instance Frances Yates describes Ficino's magic as 'gentle, artistic, subjective, psychiatric', and Pico's as an 'intensely pious and contemplative Cabbalistic magic'; but the magic of Agrippa, whom we now come to discuss, has, she says, 'terrible power implications'.[30]

At the beginning of this chapter I mentioned the correspondences between radically different types of world—the scheme which Reuchlin, *E Cabala*,[31] calls the Inferior, Superior and Supream, and which is borrowed from the Middle Ages. Bongo[32] calls these three worlds the ultramondane (of God and the angels), the celestial (of the heavenly bodies of astrology), and the sublunar (traditionally mutable, the place of change, and subject to the influence of the other two). According to Reuchlin the superior world is one of 'the superior powers, incorporeal essences, divine exemplars, the seals of the inferior world, after whose likeness the faces of all inferior things are found.' Even according to Du Bartas, a non-mystical writer, all things here below are copies of heavenly things, and the names of the constellations can be explained by reference to Biblical events (V, 140, 2, 4 ff.). And Pico reminds us in his *Heptaplus* that: 'hos tres mundos, a Moyse in tabernaculi constructione figuratos fuisse constat.' Reuchlin, Pico and Du Bartas call our attention to three types of correspondence. Reuchlin tells us that there is some kind of physical resemblance, some character given to things below by superior powers. For Du Bartas there is a kind of historical correspondence; human events are woven into the fabric of the celestial world, as the astrologer of the Fates believes; and Pico reminds us that in our artistic or religious endeavours here below we can figure forth this relationship.

Cornelius Agrippa of Nettesheim's *De Occulta Philosophia* (completed in 1510 but published in 1533, or after his *De Vanitate Scientiarum*, which prudently claimed that all sciences, including occult ones, were vain) is a failed text-book of magic—very short on actual technical procedures, but a useful compendium of occult beliefs, symbols, and signs.[33] It is composed of three books: I, on natural magic as applied in the elemental world, corresponding to physics; II, on celestial magic, corresponding to arithmetic; and III, on ceremonial magic, corresponding to theology.

We shall be concerned with Book II. According to Agrippa, mathematics are necessary to magic, for everything in nature is governed by number, weight, and measure as part of the divine plan; and thus by abstract things one may acquire celestial virtue.

> For whatsoever things are, and are done in these inferior naturall vertues, are all done, and governed by number, weight, measure, harmony, motion and light.
>
> (II, i, 167)

What is more, number is magically more efficacious than anything else, for it is part of the Pythagorean tradition to believe that, in a sense, things are in structure, number.

> For it is a general opinion of the Pythagoreans, that as Mathematicall things are more formall than Naturall, so also they are more efficacious; as they have less dependence in their being, so also in their operation.
>
> (II, ii, 170)

After all 'proportion of numbers' 'was the principall pattern in the mind of the Creator' (II, ii, 170). It is not just 'the number of Merchants buying and selling'—that was not what Boethius, Averro and Plato were talking about. (This supposed efficacy of number has some peculiar instances. 'A Serpent, if he be once struck with a Spear, dieth, if twice, recovers strength' (172). This is of course 'testified in divers authors'.)

Agrippa goes on to attest to the virtues of the various numbers, giving long and often contradictory lists of their properties, often with little clear rationale behind them. Two 'is called the Number of Science, and Memory, and of light, and the number of man, who is called another, and the lesser World' (II, v, 177), and 'it is called the number of wedlock and sexe; for there are two sexes, Masculine and Feminine, and two Doves bring forth two eggs, out of the first of which is hatched the Male, out of the second the Female' (II, v, 177). It is also evil, because of the second day of creation, and 'it is also reported that the number of two doth cause apparitions of Ghosts, and fearfull Goblins, and brings mischiefs of spirits to them that travel by night'—exactly how is not specified. He discusses nearly all the numbers by adducing a complete mixture of magical lore, ancient authority (that is the Pythagorean and Platonic tradition), and the Bible, with absolutely no means of distinction between them. But Agrippa does bring home to his reader the huge mass of accepted number lore, current in the Renaissance. His most distinctive use of the numbers is to use them as (obvious enough) grouping devices (e.g. four seasons, six rectilinear motions), and then, in diagram form, to give lists for the Infernal, Elementary and Celestial worlds, showing occult correspondences between them, always giving Biblical, astrological, theological and physical examples.

For instance, in discussing the number three (II, v) he shows how the number has a scale of meanings on different levels. The highest or archetypal meaning of three is the three-lettered name of God (given in Hebrew, God's own language), which signifies the Christian trinity of Father, Son and Holy Ghost. In the intellectual (ultramondane) world it signifies the three hierarchies of angels, that is the nine pseudo-Dionysian orders of angels grouped into threes to represent the Trinity. In the celestial world, three represents the three quaternions of the zodiacal signs of the Houses used in casting a horoscope. Agrippa divides the sublunary world into two, the elemental (physical) world in which three represents the three degrees of the elements, and the minor, or microcosmic world of man, in which three represents the three main parts of a man's body, the head, breast and belly. He also, as a 'Negromantike', finds triplicities in the infernal world, i.e. the three infernal furies, the three judges and the three degrees of the damned.

Agrippa rarely, if ever, manages to show the ground of the numerically mediated correspondences between worlds, except in the obvious case of astrological influence from the celestial to the inferior, sublunary world, when he says that 'there is no member in man which hath not correspondence with some sign, Star, intelligence, divine name, sometimes in God himself the Archetype'.[34]

He repeats a variation of the doctrine we found in Macrobius about the number seven:

> The number seaven, therefore, because it consists of three and four, joyns the soul to the body, and the vertue of this number relates to the generation of men . . . For when the genitall seed is received in the womb of the woman, if it remain there seaven hours after the effusion of it, it is certain that it will abide there for good . . . and the new-born child 'after Seaven dayes casts off the Reliques of the Navell.'
>
> (II, x, 193)

He then goes on to geometrical figures which 'also arising from numbers, are conceived to be of no less power' (II, xxiii, 253). 'Of these first of all, a Circle doth answer to unity, and the number ten' and is 'judged to be most fit for bindings and conjurations; whence they who adjure evil spirits, are wont to environ themselves about by a circle'—as we saw Faustus doing.

He summarizes Plato's doctrine in the *Timaeus*; in his assignation of geometrical forms to elements and to the heavens; in making earth 'a four square', fire a 'Pyramis' and the Heavens a 'dodecahedron'; and he gives a Pythagorean account of music, which, curiously, 'hath caused friendship between Men and Dolphins' (II, xxiv, 255). He assigns musical modes to the stars (II, xxvi), and tells us that the distances between the planets give forth tones. He gives a series of the possible ways of inscribing a man in a square or a circle (with illustrations, II, xxvii, 264), and then gives (270 f.) particular ideal proportions for the limbs. His twenty-eighth chapter is on Giorgio's topic, 'Of the Composition and Harmony of the humane soul'. For example, 'Reason to concupiscence hath the proportion *Diapason*; but to Anger *Diatesseron*' (277).

I wrote at the beginning of this chapter of the way in which the Renaissance numerological writers combined their Greek and Hebrew sources, believed in an order of the universe, and in man's dignity in comprehending it. All these themes, based on the image of man as microcosm, are magnificently brought together in the following part of Agrippa's Chapter XXVII, 'Of the proportion, measure, and Harmony of man's body', which I shall quote at length.

> Seeing man is the most beautiful and perfectest work of God, and his Image, and also the lesser world; therefore he by a more perfect composition, and sweet Harmony, and more sublime dignity doth contain and maintain in himself all numbers, measures, weights, motions, Elements and all other things which are of his composition; and in him as it were in the supreme workmanship, all things obtain a certain high condition, beyond the ordinary consonancy which they have in other compounds. From hence all the Ancients in time past did number by their fingers, and showed all numbers by them; and they seem to prove that from the very joynts of man's body, all numbers, measures, proportions, and Harmonies were invented; Hence according to this measure of the body, they framed, and contrived their temples, pallaces, houses, Theatres; also their ships, engines and every kind of Artifice, and every part and member of their edifices, and buildings, as columnes, chapiters of pillars, bases, buttresses, feet of pillars and all of this kind. Moreover God himself taught *Noah* to build the Arke according to the measure of mans body, and he made the whole fabrick of the world proportionable to mans body; from hence it is called the great world, mans body the lesse; Therefore some who have written of the Microcosme or of man, measure the body

by six feet, a foot by ten degrees, every degree by five minutes, from hence are numbred sixty degrees, which make three hundred minutes; to the which are compared so many Geometrical cubits, by which *Moses* describes the Arke: for as the body of man is in length three hundred minutes, in breadth fifty, in height thirty: so the length of the Arke was three hundred cubits, the breadth fifty, and the height thirty; that the proportion of the length to the breadth be six fold, to the heighth ten-fold, and the proportion of the length to the height about two thirds. In like manner measures of all the members are proportionate, and consonant both to the parts of world, and measures of the Archetype, and so agreeing, that there is no member in man which hath not correspondence with some sign, Star, intelligence, divine name, sometimes in God himself the Archetype.

So far we have discussed three types of numerology; the world harmony of Giorgio, the commentaries on *Genesis* of Du Bartas, and the magical system of Agrippa.

I should now like to conclude my investigation of some numerological encyclopaedic texts with a discussion of Pietro Bongo's *De Numerorum Mysteria* (edition of 1618). In this massive work of six-hundred-odd pages, not arranged into paragraphs, nor with any other perceptible logical order of exposition for the several numbers, Bongo provides us with a complete repertory of number symbolism as it would be seen by a Christian whose concern was for its sacred, rather than magical, significance.

Bongo's basic premise, as stated in his Preface, is that number is distinctive both of man's reason and of the order of the world as created by God. It is through number that the two are matched, that one is intelligible to the other. He says:

> Numerus est rationalis fabricae naturale quoddam pullulans principium: mente siquidem carentes, uti bruta, non numerant; adeoque Numerus, principium eorum, quae ratione attinguntur. . . .[35]

He who knows how to number can know all things. Bongo approves of the Pythagoreans who put all their knowledge of God, the soul, and the world into number: 'Arithmeticam sibi constituit omnium scientiarum matrem.' This is secret know-ledge, 'occultam arithmeticam', for we must not cast our pearls before swine, as was made quite clear by Plato—and not by Plato alone, for there is a tradition stemming from Aglaophemus, Philolaus and Iamblichus which preserves this knowledge. Indeed all true philosophy in its time does this. Further, Augustine, and Boethius, 'ille Romanorum Litteratissimus': 'affirmarent indubie Numerum creandarum rerum in animo conditoris principale exemplar fuisse. . . .'. ('They affirm that number was undoubtedly the principal plan in the mind of the founder of all created things. . . .') And of course, as we noted, above, Moses atticizes, and the Old Testament is written well within the Pythagorean, ultimately the Egyptian, tradition. As Alexander and Ambrose believed, Pythagoras was 'discipulus Iudaei', and Origen in his sixth book *Contra Celsum* tells us that Plato derived his inspiration from the Jews.

Thus the pedigree for Bongo's doctrine is quite what we have come to expect. Its occult features give him all the latitude in interpreting and reconciling his authorities he could need.

The astounding claim that Bongo makes (and it is made more or less implicitly by all our writers), is that without a knowledge of numerology we simply could not understand *why* there are (only) four elements and (only) seven planets. The numerologist alone has an answer to these questions, and this answer is of course not a straightforward logical one, for instance 'that's just the way things are' or 'that's just the way we happen to see (or categorize) them'. Instead a bold use of numerological argument is backed up by the hidden premise that this type of reasoning *must* be correct, because our occult knowledge tells us that this is the way a mathematizing God, himself identifiable with the Monad, or principle of number, wanted things to be. Thus there are four elements, since four is a number fit for generation: and seven is a number which begets nothing similar to itself, as is obviously the case with the immutable celestial bodies. For four is generated $(2 + 2)$, and generates (2×4) within the decad, and seven, as we know, does not. Bongo elaborates this point about the number seven, and like Capella, but not acknowledging him, he calls it Minerva. It is also the number of the Sabbath, and men should produce nothing on the Sabbath (pp. 283–4).

Bongo's second main claim is that number is essential to

theology, and he adduces 'non paucos locupletissimos (trust-
worthy) auctores' to prove this, especially Augustine, who tells us
that numbers in Scripture are 'sacratissimos & mysteriorum
plenissimos' (p. 8). His example here is the three days Jonah spent
in the whale, which prefigure the three days up to the resurrection
of Christ.

This type of Biblical exegesis is one of the main themes of the
book. Bongo relentlessly tracks down and collates with one another
what must be nearly all the numbers mentioned in the Bible.
Thus, for instance, two being the number of evil and discord, and
division, the division of the sheep from the goats of mankind at the
last judgment is prefigured by Adam, the father of mankind,
having two sons, one Abel, 'iustum', and the other Cain 'repro-
bum' (pp. 62–3). The third day is the day of grace—Moses
received the tablets of the law on Sinai on the third day, and the
day of Resurrection is also the third day (p. 104). Even the five
wounds of Christ are made to correspond to the five loaves with
which he fed the four thousand and to the five bases of Solomon's
temple.

For Bongo the world was instantaneously created (cf. pp. 22–4),
and the succession of days in the account of creation is only for
our human understanding (25, cf. 263). They are the perfect six,
as we have come to expect, for creation is perfect (268–9). In
explaining what was created Bongo takes over a lot of the Timaean
machinery—the elements are held together by arithmetical and
harmonic means (p. 199)—though he is ambiguous about this;
he gives the impression that he may only be helping us to understand the text of the *Timaeus*: 'haec autem quam utilia ad intelli-
gendam Timaei cosmopoeam.' The world is held together also by
the quaternary of amity and concord (p. 200) and 'Plato in
Timaeo ex Pythagorica doctrina ait caelum constare quattuor
elementis' (p. 239). He dutifully describes the five Timaean
regular geometrical figures and he assigns them severally to the
four elements and the heavens and then, curiously, goes on to
apply them also to the five senses (255–6).

He also, along with Giorgio and Agrippa, believes in the
hierarchy of the three worlds; 'tres condidit mundos, angelicum,
materialem, et humanum; intelligibilum, scilicet, corporeum, &
mistum' (p. 111) and these three worlds were referred to in
Moses's construction of the Tabernacle (p. 137—he refers to

Pico's *Heptaplus* for support). Everything is hierarchical, and organized in triplicities, and explained with diagrams, from the order of the angels to the order of the clergy in the church on earth. There are the usual correspondences of the celestial and sublunary worlds. The seven planets rule over and are assigned to seven organs of the body, seven metals, and seven archangels who, presumably, rule over them. Man, as we have learnt from Macrobius and Agrippa, develops in cycles of seven. This is worked out in considerable detail (pp. 296–9).

The themes so far described are absolutely central to the continuity of the Greek intellectual tradition, lightly Hebraicized. They are, as it were, the metaphysical underpinning for the imposition of numerical structures upon experience. The world is shot through with numerical correspondences, deliberately structured by a Divine Arithmetizer. But it becomes especially clear in this treatise of Bongo's that beyond this substructure numbers are not the categories through which we *experience* the world at all.[36] They are really once again for the most part classifying devices; and the basis of the classification is often, yet again, some merely analogical or metaphorical correspondence between the things classified. The ordering is in no sense scientific, but imposed, and the limits to what can be brought together in numerological correspondence seem as usual to depend mainly on the ingenuity of the compiler.

Thus, for instance, Bongo reasons that the created world is God's Decalogue:

> Nam dei scriptura & formatio in subiecta tabula, est mundi creatio (i.e. just as God with his finger wrote the tablets of the laws which were ten, so he created the universe). Decalogus autem in imagine caelisti, continet Solam, & Lunam, astra, nubes, lucem, spiritum, aquam, aerem, tenebras, ignem. . . .

And this surely rather haphazard collection is 'Caeli naturalis decalogus'. He also gives, for good measure, a further 'natural decalogue' for the contents of Earth (p. 370).

In similar fashion Bongo meditates upon the triad, 'qua nihil est uberius (more fruitful, luxuriant) ad mysticas significationes et reconditas', especially as he believes (along with so many other Renaissance thinkers, particularly Pico in the *Heptaplus*, lib. 6, to which he refers), that the vestiges of the Trinity are everywhere in creation. Thus a large part of his chapter on the number three is spent in assigning Triplicities to the three persons of the Deity, for example Substantia—Pater, Forma—Verbum, Ordo—Spiritus Sanctus. Even the movements of the planets are thus treated (p. 119–20). Hence:

$$\text{Planeta} \begin{cases} \text{Stationarius} & .. \quad \text{Pater} \\ \text{Retrogradus} & .. \quad \text{Filius} \\ \text{Directus} & .. \quad \text{Spiritus Sanctus.} \end{cases}$$

There are also trinities to be found in music (p. 178 ff.), for example Humana, Mundana, Instrumentalis; and, following Boethius, the types of singing are Diatonicum, Chromaticum, and Inharmonicam. Even the five senses will yield triplicities if we exploit a merely grammatical device:

Odoratus, Odorabile, Odoratur.

This heterogeneity affects the meaning of all of the numbers; so eight can symbolize the Cube, Vulcan and also Cybele (unacknowledged from Capella), Justice, for the usual reasons (p. 324), Judgment, 'quando finita saeculi hebdomada (i.e. in the eighth age), Dominus venerit ad iudicandum mundum', and Circumcision, which is performed on the eighth day, symbolizing the fact that in the eighth age, when we are resurrected, we shall be like angels and not propagate (p. 330).

Certain numbers however do seem to have a relatively stable core of meaning for Bongo, for instance nine and eleven, which are for him, evil numbers, and no good is to be said for them. For nine falls short of the perfection of the decad (p. 332), is the number of pain and dolour (we are referred to *Ezekiel*, 24), and the ninth psalm is the first in which antichrist is predicted.[37] Also Christ died at the ninth hour. There are indeed nine orders of angels, but there should have been the perfect ten, and after the fall of Lucifer man had to be created to fill up the gap (p. 337). This is confirmed by the parable about the woman who lost one of her ten drachmas.

He is just as hard on eleven as he is on nine, for eleven: 'has no connection with divine things, no ladder reaching up to things above, nor any merit.' As it transgresses the decad, so it transgresses the decalogue. It is the number of sinners and of penance.

(This gives him the excuse for one of his frequent digressions, a ferociously monkish attack on women (pp. 379–81).) Finally, pulling himself together, he tells us that the handspan of bastards is eleven inches.

I may have been guilty in much of this chapter of the 'fallacy of imitative form', in that I have tried to present a segment of the thought of four writers roughly in their own order, in their own words, and with their own emphases. A thematic approach, topic by topic, conflating these authors, might have been aesthetically more satisfying because less jumbled, but I wished to show how the stock of numerological lore was extended and restructured in the Renaissance in accordance with a particular range of overall strategies. Bongo, for example is almost medieval in his mania for tidying up, and in some of his prejudices. In the end he produces a handbook for preachers. If you wish to expound a Biblical text, then you will find what Bongo believes to be its most important allegorical meaning clearly expounded in his book. This is a limited aim, but carried out very thoroughly, as the expansions to the later editions of his book testify. What Bongo (and for that matter Giorgio) is doing is very simple—he takes over the vastly expanded Renaissance library, the scholarly knowledge of his time, and ransacks it in order to present in easily accessible form the information he is interested in. That is why the *Numerorum Mysteria* is still an essential reference book for the literary critic interested in number symbolism. By contrast, Giorgio's aim is more sophisticated: he is willing to skirmish with religious ortho- doxy in order to present an aesthetically satisfying ordered structure. He has a poet's instinct for analogy—not the instinct of a good poet, but at least that kind of vision which is willing to win victory on a purely verbal plane, as if he had proved by structuring his book musically, that the whole universe was isomorphic with it. He is less concerned with the external uses to which number symbolism can be put, than Bongo, while using in essence the same information as Bongo. He is obsessed with the Renaissance *topos* of Order—not order in society, as Ulysses in Shakespeare's *Troilus and Cressida*, for this is too much concerned with the active rather than the contemplative life which is Giorgio's ideal.

It is this root use of numerology as a framework of order, that ultimately cheats the supposedly most practical of these thinkers,

Agrippa, of success. He is really describing what he believes to be the case, rather than showing how the occult powers he believes in could change it. This leads one to the conclusion that numerological thought is really only successful, even within the Renaissance, in three ways: (a) as a structure to contemplate, which is the way Pico saw it; (b) as an overtly literary, allegorical means of interpretation of the scholarly literature of the time, a sort of sublime Euhemerism. Augustine and Bongo both basically proceed on this premise, although their position is complicated by their idea of history as reflected in its sacred books as proceeding according to a divinely ordained numerological plan; (c) as a serious scientific hypothesis. If there really is a harmonic framework underlying the universe, which Plato and Moses were allowed to proclaim, then actual observation ought to confirm it. It is this scientific approach which we discuss in the next chapter. We then, for the rest of the book, return to consider the practical implementation of the aesthetic consequences of the first and second views. We shall see how Renaissance artists believed that it was possible to contemplate numerologically structured aesthetic objects so that the soul of the beholder entered into a secret harmony with them, and also to interpret them as having hidden meanings which are properly aesthetic, at least in the sense that they do not make the really strong claims of a Bongo or an Agrippa to a theological or magical truth.

Notes

1 *The Elements . . . faithfully (now first) translated into the English toung by H. Billingsley, with a very fruitfull Preface made by M. J. Dee* (London, John Daye, 1570).

2 Kristeller, *Renaissance Thought*, I (1961), p. 16, cites Homer, Sophocles, Herodotus, Thucydydes, Xenophon, Isocrates, Demosthenes, Plutarch, Lucian, Epicurus, Sextus, Plotinus.

3 A word explicitly recognized to be Pythagorean, cf. e.g. Stanley, *Hist. of Phil.* (London, 1656), p. 14.

4 p. 5. 'The dictum of the philosopher Numenius is indeed well known. What is Plato, but an Athenian Moses? . . . either Plato was "Philonizing", or Philo "Platonizing", so familiar is his mode of thinking and speaking to the platonic one.'

5 Quoted by Heninger, 'Some versions of the Pythagorean Tetrad', *Stud. Ren.*, VIII (1961), pp. 7–33.

6 I am greatly indebted for much of what follows to Frances Yates, *Giordano Bruno and the Hermetic Tradition* (London, 1964).

7 Yates, op. cit., p. 2.

8 And even 'for the middle ages, Plato was not the logician nor the philosopher of love, nor the author of the *Republic*. He was, next to Moses, the great monotheistic cosmogonist, the philosopher of the creation; hence, paradoxically, the philosopher of that Nature which the real Plato so often disparaged'. C. S. Lewis, *The Discarded Image* (Cambridge, 1964), p. 52.

9 Quoted (in Latin) by Klibansky, *Continuity of the Platonic Tradition in the Middle Ages* (1939), pp. 45–7.

10 Op. cit.

11 As quoted by E. Wind, *Pagan Mysteries in the Renaissance* (London, 1958), pp. 40–1.

12 Kristeller, op. cit., p. 17–18.

13 *Harmonice mundi* (1619) *Ges. Werke*, ed. Caspar, vol. VI, p. 299.

14 Sermon to the King, 1628.

15 As quoted in *The Age of Adventure*, ed. Santillana (1956), p. 59. The passage comes from Cusa's *Of Learned Ignorance*, tr. Germain Heron (London, 1954).

16 On which see, for example, Garin, E., *Umanesimo Italiano* (Bari, 1952), p. 103 ff.

17 For a detailed investigation of the concept of world harmony, see L. Spitzer, *Classical and Christian Ideas of World Harmony* (Baltimore, 1963).

18 Cf. D. W. Robertson, 'Allegory, Humanism and Literary Theory' in his *Preface to Chaucer*, p. 286 ff. Broadly speaking, interpretations referring to the Church were called allegorical, those which pertain to the spiritual constitution of the individual were called tropological, and those which referred to the after-life were called anagogical (ibid., p. 292). But, as Robertson points out, there is nothing sacrosanct about this division. Augustine does take allegory in these four senses. Le Fevre describes many more than these four types in his Introduction.

19 In doing this Giorgio warns us that his 'harmonic alliance' will combine the separate numerical disciplines of Physics, Arithmetic, Geometry, Astronomy, Music, and Divinity.

20 C. S. Lewis, *English Literature in the Sixteenth Century excluding Drama* (Oxford, 1954), p. 541. The following references to Du Bartas are to the *Divine Weekes and Workes*, K. Joshua Sylvester (London, 1613).

21 M-S. Røstvig, *The Hidden Sense and Other Essays* (Oslo and London, 1963), p. 71, believes this *Second Sepmaine* is patterned after the last part of the *Civitas Dei*; it has four days with four subsections to each, except for the last which has five sections: i.e. seventeen, which for Augustine symbolized the ten commandments and the seven gifts of the Holy Ghost.

22 *The Colonies*, pp. 122, 129.

23 Whom he compares to the sphere in Cusa's formula: 'I, (God be praysed) know that the perfect Circle/Whose centers every-where, of all his circle/ Exceeds the circuit' (*The Ark*).

24 Agrippa, *De Occulta Philosophia* (1651), p. 185, elaborates this with a list of examples: 'Also the Egyptians, Arabians, Persians, Magicians, Mahumitans, Grecians, Tuscans, Latines, write the name of God with only four letters,

viz. thus, Thet, Alla, Sire, Orsi, Abdi, Aeos, Esar, Deus. Hence the Lacedaimonians were wont to paint Jupiter with four wings. Hence also in Orpheus his divinity, it is said that Neptune's chariots are drawn with four horses.'

25 S. Goulart, tr. Thomas Lodge, *A Learned Summary upon the famous poem of Saluste Lord of Bartas* (London, 1621), p. 248.

26 J. A. Mazzeo, *Renaissance and Revolution* (London, 1967), p. 11.

27 D. P. Walker, *Spiritual and Demonic Magic from Ficino to Campanella* (London, Warburg Institute, 1958).

28 *Works of Christopher Marlowe*, ed. C. F. Tucker Brooke (Oxford, 1910), *Faustus*, lines 76–80, 167–9, 242–7.

29 Op. cit, pp. 75–6.

30 Frances Yates, op. cit., p. 141.

31 Printed in Thos. Stanley op. cit., p. 571 ff.

32 Petri Bungi Bergomatis, *Numerorum Mysteria* (Bergamo, 1585). I am quoting from the edition of 1618, pp. 137 f.

33 According to Lynn Thorndike, *A History of Magic and Experimental Science* (6 vols., N.Y., 1923–41), vol. 5, p. 130. Agrippa met Giorgio at Padua. I quote Agrippa from the English translation of 1651. Thorndike, op. cit., p. 34, describes the book as 'vague, totally lacking in precision, and written in the pseudo-Platonic, mooning style of Iamblichus, Ficino and Reuchlin rather than the direct practical tones of Roger Bacon and Albertus Magnus'.

34 Agrippa, p. 264. His explanation of planetary magic, as Walker reminds us, op. cit., p. 90, is in fact taken almost verbatim from Ficino's *De Triplici Vita*.

35 Bongo, op. cit., p. 1. 'Number is an original natural principle of the structure of reason; however those who have no minds, like the brutes, do not number, and so number is the principle of those who are affected by reason.'

36 He does in fact make a swift obeisance to more genuine categories, i.e. Aristotles 'Predicaments', 'quibus constare putant et intelligi quae cumque in hoc conditoris orbicularis globo continentur' (p. 359). But he is more impressed that they are a perfect number, 10.

37 In his chapter DCLXVI, Bongo has fun in making Martin Luther the Antichrist, whose number is 666, that of the beast in the Apocalypse. He does this by gematria, the assignation of number values to letters, which arose out of the fact that the letters of the Hebrew alphabet are also used as numbers, thus:

M30 A1 R80 T100 I9 N40
L20 U200 T100 E5 R80 A1

adding up to 666. Though with typical impartiality he does the same for Mahomet.

Four

Scientific Numerology—the case of Kepler

> But indeed astronomy was far from being of age as yet; and Ptolemy, in an unfortunate attempt, could make others subject to despair, as being one who, like Scipio in Cicero, seemed to have recited a pleasant Pythagorean dream, rather than to have aided philosophy.
>
> Kepler, Proem to Book V of *Harmonice Mundi*[1]

In this chapter I wish to discuss the fascinating dialectic between symbolic numerology and observational data in the astronomy of the Renaissance period, particularly in the work of Johannes Kepler (1571–1630). Some Renaissance astronomers were quite consciously 'Pythagoreans' in that, like Pythagoras, they were investigating the structure of the universe in mathematical and geometrical terms. Unlike Giorgio and Agrippa, they did not seek numerical correspondences between different orders of reality (the three 'worlds'), but confined themselves within a single universe of the earth, sun, moon, planets and stars.

Up to Copernicus' *De Revolutionibus* (1543) the 'official' astronomical order of the universe was as follows: the earth was a tiny sphere suspended at the centre of a much larger rotating sphere which carried the fixed stars. The stars moved on a sphere, since the sphere was the most perfect and regular geometrical form, reflecting the measurable and unchanging regularity of their motions. Plato insists on this in his *Timaeus* (33–4):

> A suitable shape for a living being that was to contain within itself all living beings would be a figure that contains all possible figures within itself. Therefore he (the Demiurge) turned it into a rounded spherical shape, with

the extremes equidistant in all directions from the centre, a figure that has the greatest degree of completness and uniformity, as he judged uniformity to be incalculably superior to its opposite. . . .

. . . of the seven physical motions he allotted to it the one which properly belongs to intelligence and reason, and made it move with a uniform circular motion on the same spot; any deviation into movement of the other six kinds he entirely precluded. And because for its revolution it needed no feet he created it without feet or legs.[2]

The idea that the universe was spherical, and that the planets should have circular orbits, thus had a firm grip on the imagination of astronomers from Plato onwards. These were the perfect and 'best' shapes for a God-created universe. One of Kepler's major revisions of the work of Copernicus lay in his daring to say that the planets moved not on circular, but on elliptical paths. Kepler was nevertheless unwilling to give up the symbolism of the sphere. He follows Nicholas of Cusa in taking the sphere as a symbol of the Trinity, an image of God the creator. The sphere has three regions corresponding to the three persons of the Trinity, its centre being the Father, its surface the Son (sc. the 'visible body'), and the intermediate ether-filled sphere, appropriately enough, the Holy Ghost. The three persons also correspond, in the Copernican system, as Kepler had adopted it, to the central sun, the fixed stars, and the planetary system in between.[3] We saw also above that Kepler believed with Bongo and Cusa that the sphericity of the universe reflected the infinitude of its Creator.

The movement of the planets through the zodiac of the fixed stars had been accommodated since Eudoxus by a theory of concentric spheres.[4] The planets were set in rotating shells of some thickness, concentric with the earth. The thickness of the shells was designed to allow for the variation in distance of the planets from the central earth. However, eight concentric spheres of uniform motion were not sufficient, for the planets appear to turn back in their courses (Mars for instance retrogresses in the constellation Taurus). To meet this problem, two systems, one of epicycle and deferent, and the other of eccentric with moving centre, were developed. The exact origin of these systems is not known, but they were investigated and developed by the Greeks

Apollonius and Hipparchus, who worked from about the middle of the third century to the end of the second century B.C.

The first mechanism is made up of a small circle, the epicycle, upon the circumference of which the planet is located. The epicycle rotates uniformly about a point on the circumference of a second rotating circle, the deferent, whose centre coincides with the centre of the earth. The second mechanism consists of a circle with centre eccentric to the centre of the earth. This eccentric centre itself rotates about the centre of the earth, and the planet is situated on a point at its circumference. The two systems, which

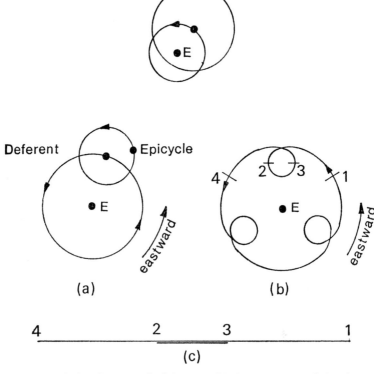

(a) typical epicycle and deferent; (b) loops generated by it approximately in plane of the ecleptic; (c) a portion of the motion of the planet as seen from the central earth, E (under both systems described in the text).

(Adapted from Kuhn, *The Copernican Revolution, p. 61*)

were in fact proved to be equivalent to one another, were, as can be seen from the diagram, simply geometrical devices designed to 'save the appearances'. They can be used, on paper, to generate the supposed path of a planet. Because of this equivalence these systems were thought of as purely conventional, and not as describing real celestial machinery. That which distinguished Kepler, marking him off from most of his colleagues, was that he was concerned with what actually happens in the heavens, in terms of a physical model, and not merely with accurate prediction of the positions of the planets, which the two geometric systems in fact accomplished fairly satisfactorily.

Systems of the planets of the kind described (highly elaborated), were dominant up to the time of Copernicus. As Kuhn says:

> the Revolution was an incredibly long time coming. For almost eighteen hundred years, from the time of Apollonius and Hipparchus until the birth of Copernicus the conception of compounded circular orbits within an earth-centred universe dominated every technically developed attack upon the problem of the planets, and there were a great many such attacks before Copernicus.[5]

As everyone knows, Copernicus produced a quite different explanation accounting for the motions of the sun, moon and planets that involved placing the sun at the centre of the universe (i.e. of the earth's orbit), thus reducing the status of the earth to that of a planet. Copernicus, and Galileo and Kepler following him, were all influenced by the humanist belief, stemming from the tradition which is the subject of this book, that the universe was mathematically ordered in a harmonically satisfying way. Indeed they produced a reading of the data that satisfied their 'ear' for mathematical harmonies. They were also influenced by a quasi-religious reverence for the sun. In some Hermetic writings the sun is the demiurge, the 'second God', and in Pythagorean and Orphic thought the sun was associated with the monad, as a key image of the deity.[6] It is also associated with truth, light, and the cosmic 'mens'. Thus Valeriano: 'Sol unus est, eadem est veritatis hieroglyphicum, duplicia enim et multiplicia sunt veritate contraria'.[7]

Thus Copernicus prefaces his highly technical *De Revolutionibus* with a suitable piece of Neo-Platonic intellectual window dressing. It is interesting to note that a work which came into conflict with the Biblical view of the earth as the immovable work of the God of the Hebrews,[8] should refer to the sun itself as a kind of pagan God:

> In the middle of all is seated the sun. For who indeed in this most beautiful temple of the universe could place the torch of the sun in a better place than one from which it can simultaneously illuminate the whole? Not ineptly indeed do some call it the lamp of the world, others its mind, others the Governor. Trismegistus calls it the visible God.[9]

He goes on to tell us how the sun sits on a royal throne, ruling his children the planets which circle around him.

Kepler gives this doctrine about the sun a typically Neo-Pythagorean mathematical twist:

> Therefore, since the sun is the source of light and eye of the world, the centre is due to it in order that the sun— as the father in the divine symbolizing—may contemplate itself in the whole surface—which is the symbol of God the Son—and take pleasure in the image of itself, and illuminate itself by shining, and inflame itself by warming.[10]

Milton takes up this idea of the sun as an eye from Ovid, and uses Pliny's name of 'mundi animus' when Adam says, 'Thou Sun, of this great world both eye and soul'.[11]

It is important to realize that Copernicus' account was intellectually more satisfying, although in fact more cumbersome than the previous ones. The data he had to explain had already been explained sufficiently to 'save the appearances'. No new observational data forcing a reinterpretation were known till some time after his death. Thus Copernicus' motives for his reinterpretation of the order of the universe have to be sought in the climate of ideas outside technical astronomy, and I would say that this climate was, for Copernicus and Galileo, and especially for Kepler, a numerological one.[12]

Copernicus indeed, may have seen himself as a Pythagorean initiate: in his prefatory letter to Pope Paul he says:

> I hesitated long whether, on the one hand, I should give to the light these my Commentaries written to prove the

Earth's motion, or whether, on the other hand, it were better to follow the example of the Pythagoreans, and others who were wont to impart their philosophic mysteries only to initiates and friends, and then not in writing but by word of mouth, as the letter of Lysis to Hipparchus witnesses.[13]

And then in his First Book of *De Revolutionibus*, which is less technical than the rest, and is directed to laymen, he produces purely Platonic reasons for the sphericity of the universe:

This is either because that figure is the most perfect, as not being articulated, but whole and complete in itself; or because it is the most capacious and therefore best suited for that which is to contain and preserve all things . . .
(and so on).

In his fourth section he goes on to argue 'that the motion of heavenly Bodies is Uniform, Circular and Perpetual, or composed of Circular Motions'.

By endowing the earth with motion Copernicus was able to explain such phenomena as retrogradation, without resorting to a complicated system of epicycles. In place of the earth-centred system of twelve circles to describe planetary motions (one each for the sun and moon, and two each for the five remaining planets) Copernicus used only seven circles, one each, sun-centred, for the six planets, and a further earth-centred one for the moon. This basic economy however is slightly illusory. In fact Copernicus had to use quite a complicated system of minor epicycles, and his explanation was, in the end, as complicated as that of Ptolemy. But, for the technical astronomer, his system did have an undeniable aesthetic appeal. He appealed to the astronomer's ear for Neo-Platonic mathematical harmonies, although his predictions were hardly better than the previous ones. It is this Pythagorean aspect of Copernican thinking that appealed most strongly to Johannes Kepler.

Kepler was a lifelong Copernican.[14] He was probably committed to the system by Maestlin, his teacher when he was a student at the university of Tubingen. His *Mysterium Cosmographicum* (1593) opens with a detailed and developed defence of

Copernicus, showing for the first time the full force of his mathematical arguments. Copernicus, however, had still allowed the orbital planes of the planets all to intersect at the centre of the earth's orbit. Kepler took the sovereignty of the sun, and the simple planetary status of the earth much more seriously, and made these orbital planes intersect in the sun. Throughout his life his 'point of view' upon the universe was that of the sun. Kepler in this book was mainly concerned to produce a post-Copernican explanation of the positions of the six circum-solar planets. On 19 July 1595, he wrote:

> If, for the sizes and relations of the six heavenly paths assumed by Copernicus, five figures possessing certain distinguishing characteristics could be discovered among the remaining infinitely many, then everything would go as desired.[15]

He was inspired to find his solution in an amazing reapplication of Plato's doctrine of the five regular solids. According to Euclid's geometry, book XIII, there were, and could be, only five solids, constructed by geometrical means, whose unique characteristics are that all their faces are identical in shape and area, only equilateral figures being used for faces. Kepler thought that by treating the planetary orbits as if they took place on solid spheres, the distance between the spheres, and hence the distance between each planet and the sun, was determinable by the insertion of one of these regular solids between the successive spheres.

> The earth is the measure for all other orbits. Circum-scribe a twelve sided regular solid (dodecahedron) about it; the sphere stretched around this will be that of Mars. Let the orbit of Mars be circumscribed by a four sided solid (tetrahedron), the sphere which is described about this will be that of Jupiter. Let Jupiter's orbit be circum-scribed by a cube. The sphere circumscribed about this will be that of Saturn. Now, place a twenty sided figure (icosahedron) in the orbit of the earth; The sphere inscribed in this will be that of Venus. In Venus' orbit place an octahedron. The sphere inscribed in this will be that of Mercury. There you have the basis for the number of the planets.[16]

Kepler also uses these geometrical objects in a fresh attempt to visualize the architecture of the universe. He does this by interposing a regular solid between two adjacent planetary orbits, so that the inner planet, when at its greatest distance from the sun, lies upon the outer surface of the inscribed sphere of its solid. The outer planet at its least distance would lie on the inner surface of the circumscribed sphere of the solid. He could just make this arrangement (e.g. by placing an octahedron between Mercury and Venus) into a useful description, but only by assuming that any discrepancies were due to the inaccuracies of Copernicus' observations.

Kepler had thus found that the relationship between the numbers supplied by the possible dimensions of the five regular solids and those which Copernicus stated for the distances of the planets from the sun practically agreed. By proving this relationship in detail Kepler could try to show, like Plato before him, that God, proceeding *more geometrico*, had a plan intelligible to men. As he said:

> the mathematical things are the cause of the physical because God from the beginning of time carried within himself in simple and divine abstraction the things as prototypes of the materially planned quantities.[17]

He further thought that since there could only be five regular solids, thus disposed, he had shown conclusively why there were six and only six planets, echoing Bongo's view that numerological arguments reveal to us the 'why' of things.

Kepler's most enduring achievement is his statement of his three laws of planetary motion. They are not in any sense number symbolic—but are yet the result of his search for a 'harmonic' relationship of numbers within the observational data. Indeed the first of these breaks away from an important 'symbolic' *a priori* assumption, that the universe is a sphere, and the paths of the planets are circular. For the first of Kepler's laws says that the path of each planet is not a circle but an ellipse, with the sun at one focus of the ellipse. This law completely eliminated the need for epicyclic motions, and represented a huge gain in simplicity.

The second law concerns the speed of the planets. Copernicus had insisted upon a constant speed of cycle and epicycle having inherited the axiom of uniform motion from Plato and Aristotle; Kepler was forced to abandon this belief, but managed to evolve a law which said that the planet would traverse equal areas of the ellipse of its orbit in equal times.

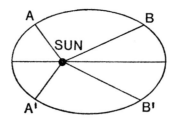

Thus, though the distances AA¹ and BB¹ are not equal, the areas SAA¹ and SBB¹ are equal. In other words, the radius vector joining the sun to a planet sweeps out equal areas in equal times. These two laws were published in 1609 in his *De motibus stellae martis.* Kepler's third law was published in *Harmonice mundi* (1619). It says that the square of the time of revolution of any planet is proportional to the cube of its average distance from the sun; that is, the ratio of the two quantities is the same for all planets. Thus one can compute the time of revolution from knowledge of the distance from the sun, or vice versa.

In this late phase of his career Kepler vastly extended his search for numerical correspondences in the universe, in his *Harmonice mundi.* In this book he attempted to erect a simple musical harmonic system for the universe. He wishes:

> To erect the magnificent edifice of the harmonic system of the musical scale, an edifice whose furnishing is not arbitrary, as one might think, not a human discovery, which one can alter, but presents itself through and through in conformity with reason and nature, so that God the Creator himself has expressed it in harmonizing the heavenly motions.[18]

Kepler thus attempts to revive the Pythagorean and Macrobian doctrine of the 'music of the spheres' in an entirely new guise. In true Pythagorean style he believes that musical harmony will provide the clue to the structure of the universe: but his conception of harmony is immensely more complicated than the Greek one.[19] With a vastly extended repertoire of musical ratios he hopes to be able to explain how all of his observational data concerning the positions and velocities of the planets, really fall within the system of musical harmony, once that is given a mathematical formulation: '. . . I grant that no sounds are given forth, but I affirm and demonstrate that the movements [of the planets] are modulated according to harmonic proportions'.[20]

His aim is also truly religious, as was that of the Greeks. His investigations are all part of a religious quest, as his frequent interpolation of prayers and invocations into his texts makes clear. His aim is 'to illustrate the glory of the world, and of God the Architect'.[21]

Indeed he repeats in *Harmonice mundi* the Platonic doctrine that 'the souls of men rejoice in those very proportions that God employed [in the creation] wherever they find them'. But he differs from Pythagoras and Plato in that he insists that it is the *speed* and not the distance of the planets from their common centre of revolution (the sun), which determines the musical celestial harmony. He calculates the range of notes that the planets give forth from the angle which the planet would appear to describe in one day as seen from the sun. Even though his system seems to be a purely mathematical one, he cannot at times resist a kind of analogical speculation: 'The Earth sings MI FA MI so that you may infer even from the syllables that in this our domicile MIsery and FAmine obtain.' He concludes:

> Accordingly the movements of the heavens are nothing except a certain everlasting polyphony (intelligible not audible) with dissonant tunings, like certain syncopations or cadences (wherewith men imitate these natural dissonances), which tend towards fixed and prescribed clauses—the single clause having six terms (like voices) and which marks out and distinguishes the immensity of time with these notes. Hence it is no longer a surprise that man, the ape of his Creator, should finally have discovered the art of singing polyphonically (*per concentum*), which was unknown to the ancients, namely in order that he might play the everlastingness of all created time in some short part of an hour by means of an artistic concord of many voices and that he might to

some extent taste the satisfaction of God the Workman with His own works, in that very sweet sense of delight elicited from this music which imitates God.[22]

Kepler believes with Proclus (cf. the latter's commentary on Euclid), that mathematical things exist apart from sensible things; that 'Geometria est archetypus pulchritudinis mundi', and that God in his creation had put his mathematical signature on things. (Kepler invokes the concept of the 'signatura rerum', as we find it in Agrippa, Paracelsus and others.)

The intuitive theory of knowledge that we have noticed elsewhere is quite explicit in Kepler. It is the soul which generates and corresponds to the harmony of the universe. Making a harmonic discovery for Kepler is:

> to uncover, to comprehend and bring to light the similarity of the proportion in sense matters with a particular prototype of a real and true harmony, a prototype existing inside the mind.[23]

Thus astrological influence itself can be explained as a kind of mathematical correspondence between soul and stars: Caspar reports that 'according to Kepler the geometrically formed soul becomes excited, when the heavenly bodies travelling on the zodiac form with each other the kind of angles which appear as angles at the centre of the regular polygons which can be constructed' (p. 278). This is indeed a highly sophisticated version of the Renaissance theme of the soul as centre of the universe.

Despite his belief in divinely ordained harmony in the universe, Kepler has a clear idea of the difference between a quantitative mathematics, and a *purely* Neo-Pythagorean, numerological and Hermetic mathematics. This crucial difference in attitudes to mathematics comes out in his controversy with the Englishman Robert Fludd.[24] Here we can see Kepler trying to free scientific mathematics from some of its numerological accretions. He accuses Fludd: 'Tu tractas Mathematica more Hermetico.' Yet, as we have seen, Kepler himself adheres to the basic premise for all such beliefs, that God made the world according to a humanly satisfying mathematical plan, which we can discover. In his *Apologia* he tells Fludd that his illustrations are 'hieroglyphics' or 'pictures' whereas his own (Kepler's) are mathematical diagrams:

Your pictures may be compared to my diagrams: admittedly my book is not so well ornamented as yours, nor is it to the taste of all readers: I excuse this defect on account of my profession: I am a mathematician.[25]

For Fludd mathematics was ultimately based on astrology and its relationships were pursuable through the three worlds, empyrean, celestial and elemental. Kepler says he is solely concerned with the celestial world:

> We come now more closely to the principles on which Robert Fludd has constructed his own cosmic music. First, he occupies the whole universe, with its three parts, Empyrean, Celestial, and Elementary. I only tackle the celestial part, and not the whole of that, but only the motions of the planets beneath the zodiac. He, trusting in those ancients who believed that the power of harmonies derived from abstract numbers, is satisfied if he can bring together in any way whatsoever, by means of numbers, those parts which he demonstrates to be a concord, not caring what clashes [sc. discrepancies with observation] are reconciled by that number. . . .[26]

Kepler and Fludd would however both have agreed with Plato that 'mathematics draws the soul upwards', and they both believed that mathematical figures were in some sense ideal. Kepler's great quest was to find satisfying relationships between them, to find the perfect harmony of a particular series. And we must not underestimate the extreme difficulty and complexity of his task, the thousands of calculations he had to make using the known observational evidence.[27] His chief satisfaction lay in seeing the correct configuration of numbers in a problem as a whole. The basic model to bear in mind in thinking of Kepler, and one which is also particularly applicable to all we shall have to say in the rest of this book, is that of a soul corresponding to and intuiting the relationships within an artistic construct. This is a kind of religious contemplation. The soul of the astronomer corresponds to the harmony in the world-soul of the cosmogonies, and this can be for him an aesthetic satisfaction, for 'Geometria est archetypus pulchritudinis mundi'.

Notes

[1] Tr. C. G. Wallis in *Great Books of the Western World*, vol. 16, Encyclopaedia Britannica (1952), p. 1010.

[2] Lee trans., pp. 44–5.

[3] Cf. e.g. *Epitome*, Bk IV, 1, 1 (Wallis trans., pp. 853–4).

[4] Their order outwards from the earth since the time of Ptolemy was accepted to be: moon, Mercury, Venus, sun, Mars, Jupiter, Saturn.

[5] *The Copernican Revolution* (New York, 1958), p. 74. I am indebted to this work in much of what follows.

[6] Cf. Fowler, *Spenser and the Numbers of Time* (1964), p. 77, which also refers us to Ficino, *Opera* (1576), vol. II, pp. 1097–8, and also Goulart's Commentary on Bartas, p. 182. Ficino wrote a *Liber de Sole*; cf. esp. the passage in *Opera*, vol. I, p. 966.

[7] *Hieroglyphica* (Frankfurt, 1613), XLIV, li, p. 555. 'The sun is one, and is thus the symbol of truth, for duplicity and multiplicity are contrary to truth.'

[8] Copernicus, in his prefatory letter to *De Revolutionibus*: 'It may fall out, too, that idle babblers, ignorant of mathematics, may claim a right to pronounce judgment on my book, by reason of a certain passage of Scripture basely twisted to suit their purpose. Should any such venture to criticize and carp at my project I take no account of them; I consider their judgment rash, and utterly despise it.' (Kuhn's translation, op. cit., p. 143.) The texts upon which the Biblical fundamentalists relied were the *Book of Joshua*, 10, 12— 'sun, stand thou still', and the 104th Psalm—'God established the earth on foundations that should not be moved for ever'. Cf. also *Job* 38. Copernicus was put on the Index in 1616.

[9] Translated from the Thorn edn (1873), p. 30. T. I. M. Beardsworth points out in his *Kepler, the Great Dane and the Bear* (forthcoming) that Copernicus may have interpreted Trismegistus as describing a heliocentric system. Cf. *Corpus Hermeticum* (ed. Scott), Book XVI, 7 and 17.

[10] *Epitome*, IV, 1, 2 (Wallis, p. 860).

[11] *Paradise Lost*, V, 171.

[12] This is disputed in the case of Galileo. He seems to dissociate himself from Neo-Pythagoreanism in his *Dialogue* (see the Salisbury translation ed. Santillana (1953), p. 15 and note). And Strong, in his book, *Procedures and Metaphysics* (1936), denies that Platonic metaphysics was the foundation of Galileo's mathematical science (cf. esp. p. 186). This is against Burtt's interpretation in *The Metaphysical Foundations of Modern Science* (London, 1949), ch. 3.

[13] As translated in Kuhn, op. cit., p. 137.

[14] It is interesting to note that Copernicus' heliocentric theory is referred to in Recorde's *Castle of Knowledge* (1556), and that it is accepted in nearly every important English text book from then on. (See F. R. Johnson, *Astronomical Thought in Renaissance England* (Baltimore, 1937, p. 291).

[15] Quoted in M. Caspar, *Kepler* (New York, 1960), p. 63.

[16] Caspar, op. cit., p. 63.

[17] Caspar, op. cit., p. 67.

[18] In Caspar, op. cit., p. 277.
[19] See pp. 1026–8 of Wallis's translation, where Elliot Carter Jr. has appended an excellent explanation of Kepler's harmonic system and its relationship to the modern one.
[20] Preface to Book IV of *Epitome* (Wallis, op. cit., p. 846).
[21] Wallis, p. 850.
[22] *Harmonice mundi*, V, 7 (Wallis trans., p. 1048).
[23] Quoted Caspar, p. 269.
[24] There is a good account of this in Pauli, W., and Jung, C. G., *The Interpretation of Nature and the Psyche* (Eng. Trans. London, 1955), in Pauli's chapter 'The Influence of Archetypal Ideas on the Scientific Theories of Kepler', p. 190 ff. Kepler in an Appendix to *Harmonice mundi* (1619) attacked Fludd, who replied in the second volume (1621) of his *Utriusque cosmi . . . historia*. Kepler answered this in his *Apologia* (1622) and Fludd replied in his *Monochordum Mundi* (1623), a work of significantly Pythagorean title. See Caspar, *Gesammelte Werke* (Munich, 1940), Band VI.
[25] I have translated from the passage quoted in F. Yates, *Giordano Bruno and the Hermetic Tradition* (1964), p. 443.
[26] Translated from *Harmonice mundi* appendix to *Werke*, op. cit., VI, p. 375.
[27] His grappling for an explanation of the orbit of Mars is especially exciting in this respect. Cf. his *De Motu Stellae Martis*, and Caspar, *Kepler*, p. 123 ff.

Five

Aesthetic Assumptions

At this point my argument has, in a sense, to begin again. In the
preceding chapters of this book I have tried to show that numerological thinking was used for broadly philosophical, cosmological
and theological ends. I have given only scattered indications of the
consequences for the aesthetic of numerological proportion,
because the writers so far discussed did not consider numerological
aesthetic to be the whole, but only a component part of their
concern, and I have wished to indicate their main strategy. But
since numerological thinking had such diverse aims and infiltrated
so many different spheres of knowledge, it is very likely that artistic
works concerned with those spheres have a numerological plan.
As various disciplines were unified through the common language
of mathematics found within them (I am thinking especially of
music, astronomy, Biblical exegesis, etc.), so also there arose the
conception, or perception, of a common bond, of symbolic import,
between such apparently disparate subjects as music and astronomy
(as in fact we saw in Kepler), music and architecture, poetry and
the Bible, and poetry and music.[1] If a Gothic cathedral is supposed to foreshadow God's Kingdom on earth, then it may well
be proportioned according to the numerical model of the Heavenly
Jerusalem provided in the Bible;[2] if a Renaissance church is supposed to be a microcosm of the whole creation, then we may well
ask if its proportions do not correspond to those of the Platonic
Lambda. In this chapter I should like to prepare the reader for
analysis of number-symbolic works of art by showing that, along
with the numerological associations of the particular disciplines of
the arts and of their subject-matter, there went a background
assumption that the basic, 'good-making', formal characteristic of

works of art were unity, proportion and harmony, which are all susceptible of a mathematical interpretation.

In fact the Renaissance period contributed little that was both original and of any importance to formal philosophical aesthetics. The subject did not attract any great thinker and no one tried consciously to add to its inherited stock of concepts, despite interminable and well worn arguments about the concept of imitation, the moral effects of poetry, the relationship between poetry and history and so on. Thus we find ourselves as before pursuing our theme across a historical gap. Later Greek and Neo-Platonist thought, with small Scholastic qualifications, provides the basic aesthetic assumptions of Renaissance artists. The Renaissance was a period of astounding creative energy; displaying all the originality and sheer inventiveness that is so lacking in the more abstract thought of the period. Thus many of the newer types of literature (especially drama) posed entirely new aesthetic problems—but as it happened, apart from what was in any case a later revival of neo-classical Aristotelianism, little attempt was made to face them. We do not know, in theoretical terms, what Shakespeare thought of tragedy, or Donne of 'metaphysical' imagery; though of course we can infer much.

Even in the Middle Ages there had been little incentive to treat the arts as offering distinctive problems. Painting and architecture belonged to the purely mechanical arts (a low status from which we see them escape in the Renaissance), and poetry and rhetoric were taught as part of the trivium, and music in the quadrivium— but this was largely a matter of technical instruction. The problem of 'the beautiful' was largely a matter of theology. (There are strong remnants of this view in the writings of Ficino.) For the foundations of Renaissance aesthetics, then, we must go back once more to the Greeks.

In what follows I shall ignore a vast amount of work in aesthetics (for example Aristotle's *Poetics*) and concentrate on the works of those thinkers who also contributed in some way to the numerological tradition. But this is not to say that these were eccentric or peripheral. There can be no doubt that they were concerned, and were often the most important thinkers concerned, with some of the basic and most generally accepted concepts of aesthetics— beauty, unity, symmetry, proportion and harmony, and also with the way in which the form of a work of art may project a world.

As noted in the first chapter, the Pythagoreans and Platonists provided the earliest of the aesthetic theories of formal beauty in so far as they believed that a numerical structure underlay both the qualitatively pleasing intervals of music, and the beautiful cosmos. They had also grasped a basic point, that the beauty of physical objects must lie in some way in the relationship of part to part within a unified whole. Proportion is all. Thus in the construction of a temple, or a vase, or in the appraisal of the human body, precise mathematical measurement may be thought to ensure a beautiful harmony in the work of art. As Plato tells us in the *Philebus* (64E): 'the qualities of measure (*metron*) and proportion (*symmetron*) invariably . . . constitute beauty and excellence.'

Plotinus later developed Plato's thought concerning beauty and symmetry and gives it a further theological twist—we do not simply contemplate a world of ideal forms when we apprehend the Beautiful; we rise through fallen matter to the contemplation of the One God. He says that 'everyone declares' that symmetry of parts constitutes beauty, and also that the soul by its very nature has a kinship to the 'noblest existents in the hierarchy of Being'. Thus he can conclude, in terms obviously derived from the *Timaeus*, that:

> harmonies unheard in sound create the harmonies we hear and wake the soul to the consciousness of beauty, showing the one essence in another kind: for the measures of our sensible music are not arbitrary but are determined by the Principle whose labour is to dominate Matter and bring pattern into being.[3]

St Augustine was also greatly influenced in his aesthetic thinking by the Neo-Platonic tradition deriving from the *Timaeus*. For him physical objects participate in the forms that exist in the mind of God by virtue of their numerical properties. He thus sees number, by which he generally means rhythm or metre, as a basic onto-logical category, and also as fundamental to beauty. He also, very unusually, takes dancing as an example:

> Suppose there is no actual work in hand and no intention to make anything, but the motions of the limbs are done for pleasure, that will be dancing. Ask what delights you in dancing and number will reply, 'Lo, here am I'.

Examine the beauty of bodily form, and you will find
that everything is in its place by number. Examine the
beauty of bodily motion and you will find everything in
its due time by number.[4]

Augustine also expressed Plotinus' view of the connection or
affinity, through order and proportion, of the lowest kind of
earthly beauty, and of heavenly beauty. Thus aesthetic contemplation can serve a religious function; like mathematics
according to Plato it 'draws the soul upwards' through a hierarchical, ordered universe, for everything is beautiful that is in due
order.[5] But aesthetic proportion does not only have this religious
function—it also unifies the work of art. For Augustine composite
things only become wholes once they are harmonized, or given
symmetry, which consists in the likeness of one part to another.[6]
These doctrines do not only apply to the visual arts, e.g. to the
artisan who produces a beautiful ('numerosus') effigy in wood,
described in *De Musica* (6,17,54), but also to music and to
poetry. Thus he praises David who:

had great skill in songs, and loved music, not out of his
private pleasure, but in his zealous faith: whereby in the
service of his (and the true) God, in diversity of harmonious and proportionate sounds, he mystically
describes the concord and unity of the celestial city of
God, composed of divers particulars.[7]

And in his *De Musica*, Book VI, which may well be one of the
chief theoretical sources of inspiration for the practice of numerical
composition in poetry, he analyses all the metrical feet of Latin
poetry in detail, showing how, when divided into arsis and thesis,
they all reduce to one of the following ratios: 1:1, 2:1, 3:2, 4:3—
except the amphibrach, 3:1, which both skips a number in the
interval of the ratio, and fails to make a consonance within the
octave, and is thus imperfect.

All these concepts are used in a highly metaphysical way, as
their ancestry in Greek thought leads us to expect. There is no
reason to believe that Augustine used these concepts extensively
in any critical sense, as tools of analysis for particular works of art.
It was for Aquinas to develop them as in some way related not
simply to our apprehension of an ideal order, but also to human

modes of sense perception within an aesthetic experience. He insists that:

> Beauty relates to the cognitive faculty; for beautiful things are those which please when seen (*pulchra enim dicuntur quae visa placent*). Hence beauty consists in due proportion; for the senses delight in things duly proportioned, as in what is after their own kind—because even sense is a sort of reason, just as is every cognitive faculty. Now, since knowledge is by assimilation, and similarity related to form, beauty properly belongs to the nature of a formal cause.
>
> (*Summa Theologica*, Q. 5, art. 4)

This is a non-transcendentalist, non-Neo-Platonic, view of the matter. The aesthetic object is especially accommodated to our apprehension of it. In being so it calms our desire for the good. 'The beautiful is the same as the good, and they differ in aspect only.'[8]

For Thomas the work of art is proportioned because the mind likes order and unity. Thus the Schoolmen speak of beauty as 'the splendour of form shining upon the proportioned parts of matter'. They recognize beauty as a category to which many things, artificial and natural, can be assigned, but they do not see it as primarily transcendental in the Platonic sense. Their idea of proportion is an empirical one.

I would choose these four thinkers, Plato, Plotinus, Augustine and Aquinas, as the best ones to exemplify the concepts which are central in the application of the numerological tradition to artistic creation in the Renaissance. Their ideas are indisputably central in any aesthetic discussion attempting to deal with our concept of the form of a work of art. It is also important to notice that they can have a further application, to our intuition of an order parallel to that of God's own creation. They are given an analogical reapplication, once we talk about the 'world' of a work of art, or of an artist's attempt to produce a microcosm of the world's order.

Thus part of Ficino's concept of beauty is tied to the idea of cosmos, and its order: 'This composite of all the forms and Ideas we call in Latin a *mundus*, and Greek a cosmos, that is *Orderliness*. The attractiveness of this *Orderliness* is Beauty'.[9] Ficino of course takes a transcendentalist, Neo-Platonic view rather than Aquinas's naturalistic one. His chief sources here are in fact Plato, Plotinus and Augustine. In particular he follows Plato's doctrine in the *Philebus* in considering that the mixture of knowledge and pleasure in the beautiful should be proportional.[10]

It will not have escaped the reader that the aesthetic concepts so far mentioned could have a quite practical application; that beyond appeasing the mind in its search for a metaphysical order or an artistic mirroring of it, the presence or absence of symmetry or proportion could be a relatively simple matter of measurement. Not surprisingly this more matter of fact view stems primarily from Rome, especially in the works of the architect Vitruvius; and in the Renaissance we find Alberti, who works in this essentially empirical tradition, using proportion and symmetry as objective standards, even guarantees, of beauty. He tries to show that our aesthetic response need not be arbitrary or unpredictable.

Alberti was a quite self-conscious classicist, making a scientific application of scientific knowledge. After his return to Florence in 1428 he was a member of the dominant artistic group under the leadership of Brunelleschi. He thus saw architecture as a civic activity—he was an early town planner. Though he respects Vitruvius, he does not take him as a final authority. His definitions of beauty in his *De Re Aedificatoria* (in ten books, probably begun about 1450; he added to it and made alterations up to his death in 1473) are roughly those of Vitruvius. But he does not simply accept harmony as an ideal—he gives an empirical criterion for it. Beauty is: 'a certain regular harmony of all the parts of a thing of such a kind that nothing could be added or taken away or altered without making it less pleasing' (Book VI, ch. 2). Alberti nevertheless further reminds us that these aesthetic concepts have to do with world order:

> Beauty is a kind of harmony and concord of all the parts
> to form a whole which is constituted according to a fixed
> number, and a certain relation and order, as symmetry,
> the highest and most perfect law of nature, demands.

There is one more crucial element in this aesthetic background— and that is the further extension of the ancient musical analogy. Alberti is

> convinced of the truth of Pythagoras' saying, that

> Nature is sure to act consistently, and with a constant
> Analogy in all her Operations: from whence I conclude,
> that the same Numbers, by means of which the Agree-
> ment of Sounds affects our Ears with delight, are the very
> same which please our Eyes and our Minds.[11]

These three quotations from Alberti give the three steps in an
argument which, as this book tries to show, was very generally
accepted in the Renaissance. (a) Works of art can be constructed
which give pleasure by virtue of their proportions; (b) these proportions can reflect laws of the constitution of nature, and (c) we
can follow Pythagoras (and hence Plato) in believing that these
proportions derived from music are of universal application, and
that (though this is very suspect) just as musical harmonies give us
pleasure when played on instruments, so they can give us pleasure
when embodied in organized lumps of matter.

   Jonson in his masque, *Loves welcome at Bolsover* (performed 1634)
satirizes the outlook of those who accept these doctrines:

> *Time*, and *Measure*, are the Father and Mother of
> Musique, you know . . . well done, my Musicall arith-
> meticall, geometricall gamesters! or rather my true
> Mathematicall Boyes! It is carried in number, weight
> and measure, as if the Aires were all Harmonie, and the
> figures well-tuned Proportion!

Jonson's satire nevertheless tends to show that this musical analogy
was a matter of common knowledge.

   Thus, to adapt a Renaissance way of thinking, the musical
analogy was pursued through three worlds—the celestial, the
physical and the little world of man. First there was the proportion
and order of creation, the 'harmony of the spheres'; then of
artifacts, taking the creation as model, which were self-subsistent
formal entities; and finally the soul of man itself, 'musicalized',
by aesthetic objects and itself musical, in the relationship of its
faculties, 'the diapason closing full in man'. Thus Du Bartas,
apropros of David's ability to quiet Saul, through music, says:

> For, if our soule be Number (some so thought)
> It must with Number be refreshed oft;
> Or, made by Number (so I yeald to sing)
> We must the same with some sweet Numbers bring

> To some good Time: even as voice (sometime)
> That in its part sings out of tune and time,
> Is by another voice (whose measur's strain
> Custome and art confirms) brought in again.[12]

Harmony, Order and Cosmos, created by God, and by the artist imitating God, were the ideals. In ordering the work of art according to ideals of proportion and symmetry one was obeying laws of nature. And furthermore, a work of art thus organized would in turn harmonize the soul of the beholder. What is remarkable about all this is its rationalism. There is no simple reliance upon the Romantic 'afflatus'—for artists and writers in this tradition creation would be a responsible business. As John Buxton reminds us, for the Elizabethan artist or writer:

> The world which he inhabited was a rationally ordered world to which his aesthetic response must also be rational. The artist therefore did not impose a human order on experience, but revealed the divine order on which it was framed; his imagination presented this in forms which would give pleasure in themselves, and his skill elicited admiration of the learning by which it had been acquired.[13]

It is further to our purpose to remember that a poet, who believed that this universe whose order he was trying to celebrate and comprehend in verse, was numerologically ordered by the Creator, might well wish to imitate Him in the form and proportion of his own work.

We come then to 'the mystical art of writing by numbers'. Certainly the relationship between music and poetry prompted poets to think of proportioning their works according to numbers symbolic of harmonic relationships. For instance Puttenham, in his *Art of English Poesie* (1589), argues that by varying the lengths of the lines and their distribution, the poet 'by measure and concordes of sundry Proportions doth counter fait the harmonicall tunes of the vocal and instrumentall Musickes'.[14] And he invokes the usual premise—since the whole world is made of number measure and weight so also should be poetry (II, 67). He cites the example of a poem fashioned to a square geometrical pattern, i.e. whose lines are equal in number to the number of syllables in each line, symbolizing constancy.[15] An example would be the envoy to Spenser's *Shepheards Calender* (= 12 × 12). This envoy is made up of twelve twelve-syllable lines (numbers appropriate to the ending of a calendar), and contains the lines:

> Loe I have made a Calender for every yeare,
> That steele in strength, and time indurance shall outware:
> And if I marked well the starres revolution;
> I shall continue till the worldes dissolution.

These lines are appropriate indeed to the virtue of constancy—content and form reinforcing one another.

Alastair Fowler, in his *Spenser and the Numbers of Time*, quotes the following passage from Minturno, *De Poeta*, ii (Venice, 1559, pp. 89–91):

> quia vero magnam in numeris vim sapientes illi veteres posuerunt, hanc perspectam esse poetis oportere . . . Doctrina autem, ac sapientia illa, quae a fonte Orpheo ad Pythagoram, ac deinceps ad Platonem permanavit, mundum musica ratione constituit. Atque cum omnis musica in vocibus, et corporis motione versetur . . . vocum autem ratio dividatur in numeros, et cantum; has omneis quidem parteis in poetica profecto reperies. Neque enim dubitandum est numeros quidem omnibus Poetis cum musicis semper fuisse communis.[16]

These remarks by Puttenham and Minturno are evidence for the belief that poetry was written in the Renaissance that was not only number-symbolic in *content* (i.e. alluded to the number-symbolic properties of numbers as do the passages from Du Bartas), but also in *structure*. We would expect that this numerological poetry would be proportioned and symmetrical and that the numbers taken for these proportions would themselves have a symbolic meaning which adds a further, allegorical, level of meaning to the manifest content of the poem. A very simple example from the *Shepheards Calender* has already been given. There is in fact further critical evidence for the practice of numerical composition. Guy Le Fevre de la Boderie, in his second introductory essay to Giorgio, which is an exposition of the technique of interpreting the scriptures in an allegorical sense, talks, as we saw, about an 'allegorie symbolique par les nombres', giving as examples the Ark, the tabernacle, etc. So far we seem to be only concerned with the interpretation of a number-symbolic content in the Bible. But Giorgio praises Ezekiel and St John for following the laws of music in their *compositions*.[17] And at the outset, in his Introduction, Le Fevre says:

> car qui ne void [*sic*] que tous les Prophetes ont esté instruits et bien appris en la vraye poesie? Qui est ce qui ne recognoist en Moyse, Ezechiel, et Sainct Jean les plus exquises & subtiles mesures de la Geometrie? Et de rechef en Moyse, Ezechiel, Daniel & St Jean les proportions des nombres. . . .

And he goes on:

> Ce sont donc ceux qu'il nous convient suivre pour nos guides: ce sont les docteurs que nous devons imiter & ceux a la mesure desquels nous devons former tout ce que nous entreprenons.

Thus Ezekiel's vision of the chariot has the structure of twenty-seven verses—the number of deity cubed: and Giorgio's own last tone of the third canto is an ode according to a musical pattern, thus fulfilling the precept of his translator.[18]

The broad outline structure of treatises was not infrequently number-symbolic. An example from Augustine was cited above.[19] Pico himself explains the structure of his *Heptaplus*. He says he follows Sts Basil and Augustine in writing seven books of seven chapters giving seven interpretations of the seven days of creation: the seventh book dealing with Christ, since He is our Sabbath, repose and happiness. His *De ente et Uno* has ten chapters as the appropriate number of the deity, when it is conceived as that which encompasses all and reduces it back to unity, as the decad does number.

However, one of the difficulties encountered by critics in detecting and interpreting number-symbolic poems, lies in the secrecy and esotericism of the numerological tradition. As Dr Fowler remarks: 'numerical composition was an essentially arcane practice in the Renaissance; so that the last thing we should expect to find is an unveiled authorial exposition'.[20]

It is partly this arcane character of the numerological tradition that has prevented critics until relatively recent times from taking proper account of number symbolism. Yet it is to be hoped that I have managed to present sufficient first-hand evidence for the reader to believe that the Renaissance artist worked in a Neo-Pythagorean intellectual atmosphere in which Giorgio, Pico and the Cabbala, with their numerological doctrines, had an important place, along with the Neo-Platonic moral thinking of men like Ficino. And there can be little doubt that English poets like Spenser and Milton, as well as Italian and French writers closer to the sources of these speculations, were fully aware of the Neo-Pythagorean tradition of thought. Once one gives full weight to the numerological tradition of exegesis upon Genesis, the Canticles, Ezekiel, Revelations and so on, all drawn from the book that formed the basis of a Christian education, then there can be even less room to doubt that the resources of numerology as described in the earlier chapters of this book lay open to the creative artist.

Notes

[1] On the very intimate relationship between (Pythagorean inspired) music and poetry in France in this period, see F. Yates, *French Academies of the Sixteenth Century* (1947), chs. III and IV.

[2] Cf. Otto von Simson, *The Gothic Cathedral* (1956), p. 35, where he says: '. . . the cathedral is perhaps best understood as a "model" of the medieval universe' and thus has a 'speculative significance' and is also an image of the Celestial City. On the Pythagorean aesthetics of the School of Chartres, see his p. 26 ff.

[3] *Enneads*, trans. MacKenna and Page (London, 1962), p. 56 I, vi, 1, I, vi, 2, p. 57, and I, vi, 3, p. 59.

[4] *De Libero Arbitrio*, II, xvi, 42, tr. Burleigh. Quoted by M. C. Beardsley in his *Aesthetics from Classical Greece to the Present* (New York and London, 1966), p. 94. I have found his section on Augustine (p. 92 ff) most useful.

[5] *De Vera Relig.*, xli, 77.

[6] Ibid., xxx, 55, xxxii, 59. Also *De Gen. ad lit. lib. imperfectus*, x, 32, cf. Beardsley, op. cit., p. 94.

[7] *Civ. Dei*, XVII, xiv, Everyman edn., II, p. 166.

[8] *Post. An.*, I–II, q. 27, art. 1.

[9] *Comm. on Symposium*, originally *De Amore*, written in 1474–5 and published 1484, I, iii, tr. Jayne, p. 128, in University of Missouri Studies, XIX, no. 1 (1944). Cf. also the way in which Ficino manipulates the concepts so far discussed in his *In Philebum* (*Opera* (1576), II), esp. chs. XXVIII, p. 1234 ff, XXV, and XXXVI, p. 1248 ff.

[10] *In Philebum*, op. cit., p. 1244.

[11] *De Re Aedificatoria*, IX, v, pp. 196–7, tr. Leoni (1726), facs. edn, London (1955). We find this latter view expressed by Boethius: 'The ear is affected by

sounds in quite the same way as the eye is by optical impressions' (*De musica*, I, 32, in Migne, *PL*, LXIII,1194).

[12] Du Bartas, *The Trophies*, op. cit. (1633), p. 197.

[13] *Elizabethan Taste* (London, 1963), p. 3.

[14] G. Gregory Smith, ed., *Elizabethan Critical Essays* (Oxford, 1937), II, p. 88.

[15] But cf. Smith, op. cit., II, pp. 94–5.

[16] Fowler, op. cit., p. 241 n. 'For indeed those ancients attributed great power to numbers, so poets too should pay attention to this . . . This doctrine, which flowed from the Orphic spring to Pythagoras and in succession on to Plato, constructed the universe on musical principles. And since all music is concerned with voices and the motion of a body, let the manner of proceeding for voices be divided into numbers and song; you will indeed find all these aspects (parts) in poetry. Nor is it to be doubted that numbers have always been held to be part of (common to) music by all the poets.'

[17] *Harmonie du Monde* (1579), p. 730 f.

[18] This is analysed by Miss Røstvig, in *The Hidden Sense*, op. cit., p. 33 ff. Cf. also the three nuptial hymns on pp. 119–21 of the 1525 Latin edition of Giorgio.

[19] Milton's *De doctrina Christiana* has 33 chapters in its first book, symbolizing the age of Christ at his death, and the second book has 17 chapters, symbolizing the ten commandments and the seven gifts of the Holy Ghost, which in turn correspond to the Old and New dispensations which form the theme of this book. He also, significantly, discusses the seven days of Creation in 1, 7, the angels in 1, 9, and sin in 1, 11.

[20] Op. cit., p. 238.

Six

Number Symbolism in England

It is just not possible in one short chapter to do complete justice to my theme; apart from anything else, so much remains to be discovered. I shall simply give brief accounts here of the influence in England of numerological ideas upon architecture and upon poetry. The texts discussed in previous chapters seem to have been known to English thinkers, although original treatises by them on numerological topics, such as William Ingpen's *The Secrets of Numbers* (1624), do not make an appearance until fairly late. John Donne, for example, refers to 'the *Harmony* of Francis George, that transcending Wit',[1] and Agrippa appears on stage in Marlowe's *Faustus* as a familiar figure, the Renaissance Magus. Further evidence of the availability of numerological ideas to English writers will of course appear as we proceed. There can be no doubt in any case of the availability of such seminal texts as Plato and the Bible: we saw these in conjunction in Sylvester's translation of Du Bartas, and I have already referred to the critical acceptance of numerological composition by quoting Puttenham's contention that the poet can in his verse 'by measure and concordes of sundry proportions . . . counter fait the harmonicall tunes of the vocal and instrumentall Musickes'.

1 Architecture and Painting

Wittkower in his book, *Architectural Principles in the Age of Humanism*, describes a number of Italian churches whose proportions embodied secret cosmic and microcosmic proportions, in support of his thesis that for the Renaissance church-builder 'the centrally planned church was the man-made echo or image of God's

universe'.[2] His book is full of information relevant to the theme
of this one: in particular concerning the aesthetics of proportion,
as we find it in such men as Vitruvius, Alberti, and Palladio. But
one example must suffice. Wittkower describes Giorgio's programme for the building of San Francesco della Vigna in Venice,
and prints his memorandum in translation in an appendix.[3] The
church was commissioned by the Doge, Andrea Gritti, who laid
the foundation stone on 15 August 1534. The architect was Jacopo
Sansovino. Giorgio's plan was to embody the Platonic Lambda in
his church, using its numbers to produce simple musical harmonies. Thus he asks for the width of the nave to be nine paces,
'which is the square of three, the first and divine number'. The
length of the nave will be 27 paces, and 'will have a triple proportion which makes a diapason and a diapente' (that is, an octave
and a fifth). He means that 27 includes the proportions 9:18:27,
which could presumably be marked by architectural features
within the church, 9:18 being the diapason (1:2), and 18:27 being
the diapente (2:3). These proportions are explicitly chosen as
being microcosmic, and in the two quotations which follow we
can see the extent to which the Demiurge of the *Timaeus* was assimilated to the Christian God the Father: for Giorgio reminds us
that: 'this mysterious harmony is such that when Plato in the
Timaeus wished to describe the wonderful consonance of the parts
and fabric of the world, he took this as the first foundation of his
description . . .', and further: 'We being desirous of building the
church, have thought it necessary, and most appropriate to follow
that order of which God, the greatest architect, is master and
author.'

Giorgio goes on to quote the Biblical precedent of the Tabernacle of Moses, which presumably intimated sufficiently clearly
to him God's interest in architectural matters. In making his
plan, Giorgio also shows how human creation may correspond to
the Universe as a whole, in its proportions. He must limit himself to
27 in constructing ratios, because Plato would not go beyond this
number in the *Timaeus*. (We remember that it was in fact chosen
as a cube, to symbolize solidity.) This is a strict rule, and Giorgio
gives strong reasons for it: 'whosoever should presume to transgress
this rule would create a monster, he would break and violate the
natural laws.' In saying this he is proceeding on essentially similar
assumptions concerning natural, that is binding, laws, as did

Kepler, and is also making a direct transition in his thought from the natural beauty of the universe to that of an artefact.

There is another kind of proportion for him to embody in his church: quite literally. For the church will contain the ideal proportions for a man. Thus he wishes the breadth of the cappella grande to be six paces, 'like a head, joined to the body proportionately and well balanced'. And in specifying the dimensions of all the other parts of the church, choir, chancel and transept, he reminds us of the musical harmonies involved. 'Thus all the measurements of the plan, lengths as well as widths, will be in perfect consonance, and will necessarily delight those who contemplate them, unless their sight be dense and disproportionate.' Like St Thomas, Giorgio appeals to the very constitution of our senses as correspondent to the beauty of proportion. Wittkower draws attention to the fact that the three distinguished men who were consulted about this memorandum showed no undue surprise, and approved of it. They were the architect Serlio, the humanist Fortunato Spira, and the painter Titian.[4]

We find nothing upon quite this scale of elaboration in England, in stones and mortar, though Spenser's fictional Castle of Alma in the *Faerie Queene* is considerably more complicated.[5] Nevertheless a curious example of a numerologically inspired building in this country is the Triangular Lodge, built in 1593 for Sir Thomas Tresham, a Roman Catholic recusant, in Rushton, Northamptonshire.

Sir Gyles Isham described this building as 'a pious conceit—almost a folly'.[6] It is meant to symbolize the doctrine of the Trinity, each of its three walls being devoted to one of its Persons, partly by means of appropriate quotations inscribed on them. It is also a pun on Sir Thomas' own name, and is decorated with the trefoil of his own arms (itself a symbol of the Trinity). Emphasizing the piety of Tresham's intention, the legend MENTES TUORUM VISITA, the second line of the hymn to the Holy Ghost, 'Veni Creator Spiritus', runs right round the building over each of the topmost windows. The walls were also adorned with numbers. Sir Gyles reports that:

> Miss Jourdain suggested on the basis of a book *Prognostication for the year of Our Lord LXXVI made . . . by John Securis*, dated *Anno Mundi* 5538, that the 55.55 over the

door represents the date of the building A.D. 1593
(i.e. Creation 3962 B.C. + A.D. 1593). In a similar way,
the other dates record, according to her, the Deluge,
the Call of Abraham, the Death of the B.V.M., the date
of the Passion.[7]

So far as I can tell from the measured architectural plans by
Gotch,[8] the dimensions of the lodge are number-symbolic. The
lengths of the walls on the ground plan are each 33' 4", and three
of these would add up to 100', a number appropriate to Tresham's
trinitarian scheme. For just as in numerological lore multiples of
ten were held to reduce or return all numbers to unity, the monad
of God, so the three Persons of the Trinity, symbolized on each of
the three walls, become mystically one, when the dimensions for
the walls are added together.

The frieze of the entablature on the upper story bears three
legends, one to a side, each legend containing 33 letters, the
lengths of the sides in this story being 33 feet. Each of the legends
refers to Christ, who is supposed to have been crucified in his
thirty-third year. The legends read: 'Aperiatur terra et geminet
salvatorem', 'Quis separabit nos a charitate Christi', and 'Con-
sideravi opera tua domine et expavi'. This last seems to have little
to do with Christ. (It is an expansion of *Habakuk* 3:2.) But as
Sir Gyles Isham points out, it is part of the Tract for the Mass of
Good Friday, and so is doubly appropriate both to Christ and to
the number symbolizing his death.

The comparative lack of buildings in England in the Italian
Renaissance style (at least, contemporaneously with the Italian
Renaissance), may be in some measure due to the fact that the
Protestant reformation largely cut England off from immediate
participation in papistical Italian developments. Henry Wotton,
however, by virtue of his diplomatic status, was perhaps better
acquainted than many of his countrymen with the artistic achievements of Catholic Europe. In 1624 he published a charming and
unassuming book which he entitled *The Elements of Architecture*.
He claims in his preface to be 'but a gatherer and disposer of
other men's stuffe', and takes as his principal master Vitruvius.
But he also admires Leon Battista Alberti the Florentine, for
having been able to conjoin mathematics and grammar, 'there
being betweene *Arts* and *Sciences*, as well as between *Men*, a kinde

of goode fellowship, and communication of their *Principles*'. Wotton thus shows himself aware of the new status of architecture as allied to the liberal arts, and also open to the idea of the unification of disciplines through the common language of mathematics found in them, which was so strongly fostered by the numerological tradition.

He is not, however, of a particularly theoretical turn of mind, and is mainly concerned to give good practical information, the 'Chief Remembrances' for the Englishman building his country house: 'First then concerning the *Foundation*, which requireth the exactest care; For if it happen to dance, it will marre all the mirth in the House.'[9] But he does seem to be aware of the numerological aesthetic, for instance when he tells us of the Church of Santa Giustina at Padua:

> In truth a formed piece of good Art, where the Materials being but ordinarie stone, without any garnishment of sculpture, doe yet ravish the Beholder (and he knows not how) by a secret *Harmony* in the *Proportions*.[10]

He certainly is thus aware of the secrecy of the Pythagorean tradition: and very possibly he knew from Alberti what the means of the ravishment were. For it depended upon the Platonic concept of a correspondence between the very structure of the soul, and harmony in the object, mediated by the Timaean harmonic numbers. This response is simply innate; thus Alberti tells us, 'Sed nature sensu animis innato quo sentiri diximus concinnitas. . . .'[11]

It is when he comes to tell us about doors and windows that Wotton summarizes, elegantly and concisely, though with some caution, the Neo-Pythagorean doctrine.

> These *In Lets* of *Men* and of *Light*, I couple together because I find their due Dimensions, brought under one Rule, by *Leone Alberti* (a learned searcher) who from the Schoole of *Pythagoras* (where it was a fundamentall *Maxime*, that the *Images* of all things are latent in *Numbers*) doth determine the Comeliest Proportion, betweene breadths and heights; Reducing *Symmetrie* to *Symphonie*, and the *harmonie* of *Sound*, to a kind of harmonie in *Sight*, after this manner: the two principals of Con-

sonances, that most ravish the Eare, are by consent of
all Nature, the *fift*, and the *Octave*; whereof the first riseth
radically from the proportion, betweene *two* and *three*.
The other from the double *Intervalle*, betweene *One* and
Two, or betweene *Two* and *Foure* etc. Now if we shall
transport these proportions, from Audible to visible
Obiects; and apply them as they shall fall fittest (the
Nature of the Place considered) Namely in some
Windowes, and *Doores* the Symmetrie of *Two* to *Three*, in
their Breadth and Length; In others the double as
aforesaid; There will indubitably result from either, a
gracefull and *harmonious* contentment, to the Eye, which
speculation through it may appear unto vulgar *Artizans*,
perhaps too subtile, and too sublime, yet wee must
remember, that *Vitruvius* himeselfe doth determine many
things in this profession, by *Musicall* grounds, and much
commendeth in an *Architect*, a *Philosophical* Spirit; that
is, he would have him (as I conceave it) to be no super-
ficiall, and floating Artificer; but a *Diver* into *Causes*,
and into the *Mysteries of Proportion. . . .*'[12]

Thus the purely empirical strain in Wotton, acceptable to 'vulgar
Artizans' gives way to the speculative, commending in the
architect a 'Philosophical Spirit'.

Some thirteen or fourteen years after the publication of Wotton's
treatise, the first Lord Fairfax began to build the second Nun
Appleton House, which was completed in about 1650. Marvell,
in his poem 'Upon Appleton House, to my Lord Fairfax' meditates
upon propriety and decorum in architecture. In doing so he
accepts in particular two principles asserted by Wotton, that man
is 'the Prototype of all exact *Symmetrie*', and (following Palladio)
that 'the principall entrance was never to be regulated by any
certain dimensions, but by the dignity of the master'. Thus
Marvell asks:

> Why should of all things Man unrul'd
> Such unproportion'd dwellings build?
> The Beasts are by their Denns exprest:
> And Birds contrive an equal Nest;
> The low roof'd Tortoises do dwell
> In cases fit of Tortoise-shell;

> No creature loves an empty space;
> Their bodies measure out their place. (st II)

Which is an argument 'from Nature', as it were. But Marvell extends it to make a moral point, in commending Nun Appleton:

> . . . all things are composed here
> Like Nature, orderly and near:
> In which we the Dimensions find
> Of that more sober Age and Mind,
> When larger sized men did stoop
> To enter at a narrow loop;
> And practising, in doors so strait,
> To strain themselves through *Heavens Gate*. (st IV)

This emphasis upon the proper relationship of a building to the dignity of its master reminds us of Pope's description of Timon's villa in his *Epistle to Burlington*: here, it seems, the Renaissance ideal of decorum has been forgotten, where the master's

> . . . building is a town,
> His pond an ocean, his parterre a down:
> Who must but laugh, the master when he sees,
> A furry insect stirring at a breeze!

At Appleton House, on the other hand, profounder principles apply. For did not Vitruvius say, in the Introduction to his Third Book: 'Namque non potest aedis ulla sine symmetria atque proportione rationem habere compositionis, nisi uti ad hominis bene figurate membrorum habuit exactam rationem.' And equally impressive was the passage in Isaiah, 44, 13: 'The carpenter stretcheth out his rule; he marketh it out with the compass, and he maketh it after the figure of a man, according to the beauty of a man.'

Marvell adverts to just this microcosmic principle of proportion, confirmed by Holy Writ, when he observes that:

> *Humility* alone designs
> Those short but admirable lines,
> By which ungirt and unconstrain'd
> Things greater are in less contain'd.
> Let others vainly strive t'immure
> The *Circle* in the *Quadature*!

> These *Holy Mathematicks* can
> In ev'ry Figure equal Man. (st VI)

Not only were buildings supposed to reflect the little world of man: but the representation of the human body itself, was supposed to be properly proportioned. Dürer was especially influential in taking this view, which we shall shortly find also in Lomazzo.[13] But his ideas were not very well received in England—in fact Francis Bacon, as a true empiricist, gives them a rather frosty reception. In his essay *Of Beauty* he dismissed Dürer as a 'trifler' who would make a personage by geometrical proportions, which Bacon supposes 'would please nobody but the painter who made it', for 'there is no excellent beauty but hath not some strangeness in the proportion'. And Hilliard, the miniaturist, although he says there are three elements in formal beauty, complexion, favour and good proportion, and grace in countenance, yet goes on to say we judge good proportion instinctively and not by Dürer's rules.[14] John Donne, as ever sceptically aware of these developments, thus makes fun of the foppish courtier who tries to regulate his own day-to-day appearance in this way, before calling on his mistress:

> Would not Heraclitus laugh to see Macrine,
> From Hat to shooe, himselfe at doore refine,
> As if the Presence were a Moschite, and lift
> His skirts and hose, and call his clothes to shrift,
> Making them confesse not only mortall
> Great staines and holes in them; but veniall
> Feathers and dust, wherewith they fornicate:
> And then by *Dürers* rules survay the state
> Of his each limbe, and with strings the odds trye
> Of his necke to his legge, and wast to thighe;
> So in immaculate clothes, and Symetrie
> Perfect as circles, with such nicetie
> As a young Preacher at his first time goes
> To preach, he enters, . . .[15]

In the face of all this distrust, it is surprising to find that Hillard was in fact persuaded to write his treatise by one Richard Haydocke, a fellow of New College, who made a translation of Lomazzo's *Trattato della pittura*, which was published in Oxford in

1578.[16] Haydocke's translation is worth examining here as further evidence of the presence of number-symbolic thinking in England.

For Lomazzo, painting is 'the very Ape of Nature' (p. 14), which imitates and expresses the passions of the mind. It is an art based on geometry, for '*Quantitie Proportioned* is the matter of Painting' (p. 18). For that reason it is a liberal not a mechanical art, for nobody calls geometry mechanical. Lomazzo thinks of his geometry in the way of Plato, with the regular solids corresponding to the elements; thus conically designed paintings are the most beautiful, as they are like fire, and ascend to their proper sphere (p. 17). Nothing can satisfy the eye without proportion, which is musical, cosmic and microcosmic in character. For head, nose and chin may be in triple proportion, which, like Giorgio's church, he holds to make 'a diapente and a Diapason' (p. 33); and the measures of all the parts of a design may be 'truely symmetrical, and correspondent to the partes of the world' (p. 35). His chapter XXX has a theme very familiar to us, for it shows how 'the measures of Ships, Temples, and other things were first drawne from the imitation of man's bodie'. Lomazzo becomes wildly over-elaborate however, and lays himself open to the ridicule of men like Bacon and Donne, when he gives recipe after recipe for particular proportions, for example for bodies of 10 heads high, 8 heads high, 7 heads high, and so on.

This latter kind of proportion is peculiarly lacking in any kind of intellectual stimulus: its speculative value peters out into a rather sophisticated version of playing with bricks. In England at least, the true complexity and fascination of the numerological tradition is reflected, not in these visual arts, but in our literature.

2 *Poetry and Music*

> Mystical grammar of amorous glances;
> Feeling of pulses, the physic of love;
> Rhetorical courtings and musical dances;
> Numb'ring of kisses arithmetic prove;
>> Eyes like astronomy;
>> Straight limbed geometry;
>> In her art's ingeny
>> Our wits were sharp and keen.
>> Never Mark Antony

Dallied more wantonly
With the fair Egyptian queen.

John Cleveland[17]

Cleveland here alludes wittily to the 'straight limbed Geometry' of Cleopatra, and this may have come from Lomazzo; but there is more to it than this. In discussing the numerological poetry of the English Renaissance we shall indeed find 'musical dances', in Davies's *Orchestra* and 'numb'ring of kisses', in Shakespeare's *Venus and Adonis*, and in much more besides. For Cleveland's satire on 'Love à la Euclid' comes towards the end of a period of Elizabethan and metaphysical poetry, in which authors were perfectly attuned to the seeking of correspondence between things apparently unlike, and more willing than at any time since in English poetry, to accept the influence of non-literary disciplines, such as music, cosmology, astrology and astronomy upon their writing. What is more, the correspondences they believed in were the literary expressions of that harmonious world view, in which all things were held to be interconnected, such as we have found in Pico, Agrippa and Ficino. All the poets whose work is to be discussed were willing to combine their chosen myth with some discipline or disciplines expressive of order, and the art of reading them thus depends to a considerable extent upon our knowledge of the intellectual tradition described in this book.

J. A. Mazzeo, in an article upon the theorists of the conceit, such as Gracian, and Tesauro, makes a generalization about this Renaissance poetic of correspondence, which is relevant here. It is true not only of those poets like Donne and Cowley, whom we think of as using the 'metaphysical' image, but also of Spenser and Shakespeare. He says:

> The definition of the conceit as the expression of the correspondences between objects . . . reveals the point of contact of this critical movement with certain aspects of the scientific and philosophical methodology of the Renaissance. The theory of the conceit seems to be, in part, the application of the principle of universal analogy and correspondence to the problems of literary criticism and poetry. The notion of cosmic affinities has, of course, a long history, but I think it is safe to say that it domi-

nated the intellectual life of the Renaissance more than
that of any other period.[18]

A small part of this history of cosmic affinities has been documented in earlier chapters. We have now to do with those learned
poets who were aware of and excited by these affinities, not only
the occult ones, but also those scientific ones involved in the
astronomical revolution. It is essential to remember also, what has
been emphasized by all writers on this period, and so many within
it that the universe is thought of by them as ideally hierarchical
and ordered.

This ideal of order, combined with the aesthetic of proportion
discussed in the previous chapter, lies at the centre of Donne's
First Anniversary. Poets of the late sixteenth and early seventeenth
centuries had to grapple with the new astronomy. Sir Thomas
Browne's Helix had indeed enlarged, and men had had to come
to terms with a vastly expanded universe.[19] This the ordinary
man in England did remarkably well. For the wide circulation of
popular books based on the new science tends to show that there
was no gap as yet between artistic and scientific world views.[20]
The men of the Renaissance found it fairly easy to embody newly
discovered scientific facts and beliefs in their poems, even if they
mourned at the same time the loss of the old symbolism, as we
shall see Donne doing. Indeed in discussing numerologically structured poetry we shall see how the numbers involved in astronomy
were quite naturally incorporated into poetry, especially as a
means of expressing that temporal sensibility, centring on the
concept of mutability, which is so typical of the period, and which
even led to the idea that the universe itself was running down,
decaying. It is only since the seventeenth century that poets have
felt that scientific ideas have cut them off from an unassimilable
way of thought: and this does *not* seem to be due simply to the
increasing degree of technicality in scientific thinking, the inherent
difficulty of its concepts and of the mathematics needed to manipulate them. For as Alastair Fowler has abundantly shown, a poet
like Spenser was well up to the most technical aspects of astronomy,
and well able to use them to impart a further allegorical dimension
to his myth.

John Donne, as is well known, was much troubled by these
developments: yet as we shall see, he uses the theme of 'all

coherence gone' in his *First Anniversary* in apposition to his main
theme, which is to eulogize Elizabeth Drury (or perhaps, The
Ideal of Woman) as the ideal of beautiful, integrated proportion.

Louis Martz, in his essay, 'Donne In Meditation; the Anniver-
saries', argues that Donne's *First Anniversary* is a carefully structured meditation, divided into an introduction, a conclusion, and
five intervening sections.[21] These sections are each subdivided
into three; (1) a meditation on the frailty and decay of the
world, (2) an eulogy of Elizabeth Drury as an ideal of human
perfection, and (3) a refrain, introducing a moral. This formal
analysis of the poem I accept, and despite Martz's pleas for consideration of the poem as a whole (somewhat defeated by his
admission that the poem lacks organic form, and in fact falls into
sections), I wish to concentrate here on the second and third
meditative sections (lines 191–246, and 247–338).

The main ideas of these sections can only be understood in the
light of the numerological tradition and its aesthetic. This is a
paradox, in so far as the theme of the second section is a flat
contradiction of the view that the universe is harmoniously
ordered and man is in tune with it:

> . . . as mankinde, so is the worlds whole frame
> Quite out of joynt, almost created lame.
>
> (191–2)

This can only have seemed an almost blasphemous hyperbole to
its audience. But it seems mainly to be directed not against the
basic assumption of harmonious world order, but against the
confusions produced by the newly assimilated Copernican world
scheme, which, as we saw, even Du Bartas felt himself called upon
to try to refute in a poem otherwise very hospitable to traditional
astronomy. Perhaps what was threatened above all was the
Timaean world scheme, with its immutable eternal, and reasonable circular motions. For:

> . . . new Philosophy calls all in doubt,
> The element of fire is quite put out;
> The Sun is lost, and th' earth and no mans wit
> Can well direct him where to looke for it.
> And freely men confesse that this world's spent,
> When in the Planets, and the Firmament

> They seeke so many new; they see that this
> Is crumbled out againe to his Atomies.
> 'Tis all in peeces, all cohaerence gone;
> All just supply, and all Relation. (205–14)

The 'crumbling out againe' of the world into Atoms recalls to mind the original opposition in ancient times between Plato and Democritus. Cornford describes the Leucippian and Democritan atomistic systems, which Plato so much opposed, in terms which might even be a gloss on Donne:

> the cause of motion seems to have entirely disappeared. Matter or body has been reduced to tiny impenetrable particles of solid 'being'. These and the void or 'not being' in which they move are the sole realities in the universe. Rational design or purpose has no part in the formation of the world. The atoms move unceasingly in all directions. . . . [they form vortices of atoms of similar size] . . . and so finally worlds are always being formed, innumerable worlds scattered throughout the void, holding together for a time and then shattered and dispersed.[22]

But the succeeding eulogy (219–36) turns this whole vision of a diseased and broken world around. Elizabeth Drury is hyperbolically praised for alone having had the power to unify all this by 'Magnetique Force' (something which, according to the new astronomy, was precisely done by the sun). But

> Shee, shee is dead; shee's dead; when thou knowst this
> Thou knowst how lame a cripple this world is.

Thus this section concludes with a play on the term 'world's beauty', to mean both Elizabeth Drury, and the old scheme:

> For the world's beauty is decai'd, or gone,
> Beauty, that's colour or proportion.

This leads Donne to a rather petulant attack on astronomy: since the spherical forms of the heavens, which for Plato symbolized Reason in the World Soul, are gone:

> We thinke the heavens enjoy their Sphericall,
> Their round proportion embracing all.

> But yet their various and perplexed course,
> Observ'd in divers ages, doth enforce
> Men to finde out so many Eccentrique parts,
> Such divers downe-right lines, such overthwarts,
> As disproportion that pure forme. (251–7)

But this is not an attack on anything new, any more than Milton's very similar complaints in *Paradise Lost*, Book VII (lines 75–84). For as we have seen, the system of eccentrics and epicycles to which Donne alludes, goes back a long way. (Though one cannot help wondering whether Donne was not very up to date, and aware of Kepler's arguments for elliptical orbits.) Donne substantiates his case by reminding us of some peculiar facts about the sun:

> . . . nor can the Sunne
> Perfit a Circle, or maintaine his way
> One inch direct; but where he rose to-day
> He comes no more, but with a couzening line,
> Steales by that point, and so is Serpentine: . . .
> So, of the Starres which boast that they do runne
> In Circle still, none ends where he begun.
> All their proportion's lame, it sinkes, it swels.
>
> (268–77)

Coffin is surely right when he says that the sun appears to take a 'serpentine' course due to a variation in the obliquity of the ecliptic;[23] but the sun also fails to complete a circle, because in its apparent diurnal journey round the earth, it in fact returns after twenty-four hours to a point in the Zodiac short of where it started, thus traversing in effect only 359 degrees.

Donne then returns for the second time to draw the contrast between the lack of proportion in the universe and its perfect embodiment in Elizabeth Drury. (Lines 305–36). Here he makes it even more explicit that he is using the concept of proportion in our sense, for he employs the topos of man as the microcosmic prototype of all beautiful symmetry and proportion, and of the soul as harmonically constituted:

> And, Oh, it can no more be questioned,
> That beauties best, proportion, is dead,
> Since even griefe it selfe, which now alone

Is left us, is without proportion.
Shee by whose lines proportion should bee
Examin'd, measure of all Symmetree,
Whom had that Ancient seen, who thought soules made
Of Harmony, he would at next have said
That Harmony was shee, and thence infer,
That soules were but Resultances from her. . . .

And he goes on to say that she could have been a 'type' for the construction of the Ark according to man's proportion (lines 317-9).

Perhaps a more charming and less hysterically praised lady is Thomas Campion's Laura. Campion's lyric to her is deceptively simple, perfectly graceful: it seems to be just the very best turned of courtly compliments, with none of the 'lumbering gear' that Donne brings to bear in his *First Anniversary*. But behind it lies a tradition of thought that stretches all the way back to Pythagoras:

> Rose cheekt Laura, come
> Sing thou smoothly with thy beauty's
> Silent music, either other
> Sweetly gracing.
>
> Lovely forms do flow
> From concent divinely framed:
> Heaven is music, and thy beauty's
> Birth is heavenly.
>
> These dull notes we sing
> Discords need for helps to grace them;
> Only beauty purely loving
> Knows no discord.
>
> But still moves delight,
> Like clear springs renewed by flowing,
> Ever perfect, ever in them-
> Selves eternal.

I leave the reader to appreciate this beautiful lyric without the clumsiness of further explanation. Nevertheless it leads us to consider the close numerological connections between music and poetry in Renaissance England. We remember how at the very beginning, the Pythagorean reverence for number stemmed from a musical discovery, and music was associated with number ever since, from the Greeks, through Boethius' *De Musica*, to Athanasius Kircher's *Mursurgia Universalis* of 1650. English writers were not only fascinated by the relation of harmony to number, but also by two favourite topics of *musica speculativa*: the celestial music of the *Somnium Scipionis*, and the effects of music on the soul, as affirmed by Plato in the *Timaeus* (47A ff.), and as symbolized in the stories of Orpheus and Amphion in legend, and of David in the Bible. These all gave rise to a number of Renaissance scholarly texts on music, though there is no English writer to compare, as a theorist, with the Italians such as Ficino and Zarlino.[24]

Of course the practice of music had progressed beyond the bounds set for it by Greek and early Medieval writers. Harmony was thought of in the modern sense, as consonance, and not as a discrete series of pleasing 'proportionate' intervals. Though harmony even in this modern sense had its Platonic allegorical analogues in the notion of harmony as the reconciliation of opposites (*concordia discors*),[25] and was thought of in this way by Renaissance theorists even when they considered the Greek tradition as passed on by Boethius, Isodore, and others. As Pattison points out,[26] Thomas Campion was the first Englishman to state the harmonic ideas that were coming to replace the contrapuntal theory of the Middle Ages. His book on counterpoint implies progression in chords, not the harmony of rhythmically independent melodies. Nor were the original Pythagorean intervals still sacrosanct. For example Lodovico Fogliano of Modena, in his *Musica Theoria* (1529), protested against the authority of the Pythagorean (6:8:9:12) consonances, and says that we actually experience the minor (5:6) and major (4:5) third, the minor (5:8) and major (3:5) and major (4:5) third, the minor (5:8) and major (3:5) sixth, the minor (5:12) and major (2:5) tenth and the minor and major sixth above the octave (5:16 and 3:10) as consonances.[27] Kepler, as we have seen, used a vastly extended harmonic series some time later, in seeking out planetary harmonies which although extended in scope, were still based on Pythagorean premises of order. But almost contemporaneously with him, in 1618, Descartes published his *Compendium Musices*, a work which did entirely without the accretions of metaphysical and cosmological lore of the numerological tradition.

Gosson, however, in his *School of Abuse* (1579) would have had

no sympathy for such practical developments. He believed that
the speculative branch of music was the only one of any worth:

> *Pythagoras* bequeathes them a Clookebagge, and con-
> demnes them for fooles, that iudge Musick by sounde
> and eare. If you will bee good Scholars, and profite well
> in the Arte of Musicke, shutte your Fidels in their cases,
> and looke up to heaven! the order of the Spheres, the
> infallible motion of the Planets, the iuste course of the
> yeare, and varieties of seasons, the concorde of the
> Elementes and their qualities, Fyre, Water, Ayre,
> Earth, Heate, Colde, Moysture, and Drought continuing
> together to the constitution of earthly bodies and
> sustenance of every creature.[28]

These are strong claims, and they are echoed sixty years later by
Sir Thomas Browne in his *Religio Medici*, when he tells us that
music is 'an Hieroglyphicall and shadowed lesson of the whole
World, and creatures of GOD: such a melody to the ear, as the
whole World, well understood, would afford the understanding'.
He even claims to experience this quasi-mystical effect, when he
goes so far as to say that 'even that vulgar and Tavern Musicke—
strikes in me a deep fit of devotion, and a profound contemplation
of the First Composer'.[29]

This musical-cosmic parallel was one of the basic metaphors
for these writers when they thought of the beauty of the universe.
John Donne accepts this, when he says that 'God made this whole
world in such a uniformity, such a correspondency, such a con-
cinnity of parts, as that it was an instrument perfectly in tune'.[30]
Fludd takes this quite literally in his *Utriusque cosmi . . . historia* in
which we find a picture of the whole of creation, supposedly
encompassed by the single string of the Pythagorean monochord,
which runs from the earth through the elements and the planets
up to the hand of God which reaches out from a cloud to tune it.[31]
We shall now find that these musical cosmic parallels are drawn
as assiduously in the poetry of the period as in speculative
philosophy and theology.

Sir John Davies's *Orchestra* (1596) is treatise-like in that it projects a world picture, using the image of a completely musicalized
universe. In Davies's myth Antinous has to persuade Penelope to
dance: and the direction of the poem lies in the omnipresent

argument of the period, that man should correspond to and co-operate with the world order. Davies admits that his story is to some extent a spurious one, for he gently chides Homer for not doing justice to Antinous, 'that fresh and jolly knight', and presumes to interpolate his pleas with 'Gentle art and cunning courtesy' into Homer's narrative, for:

> The courtly love he made unto the queen
> Homer forgot, as if it had not been.

Thus Antinous tries to make Penelope dance with him, and begins his argument with that appeal to antiquity which comes so naturally in this period: for through Plato, Antinous can go right back to the beginning of things:

> Dancing, bright lady, then began to be
> When the first seeds whereof the world did spring,
> The fire air earth and water, did agree
> By Love's persuasion, nature's mighty king,
> To leave their first discorded combating
> And in a dance such measure to observe
> As all the world their measure should preserve.

The four elements had long been supposed to be combined amicably in musical proportion.[32] They were in fact a prime example in the natural world of the *concordia discors*. Plato speaks of the elements as being in amity (*Timaeus* 32 B-C), and Spenser develops hints from Plato and from Iamblichus to make the tetrad, as a symbol of friendship, one of the master images in the fourth book of the *Faerie Queene*.[33] Davies continues his image to include the heavens:

> The turning vault of heaven formed was,
> Whose starry wheels he hath so made to pass,
> As that their moving do a music frame,
> As they themselves still dance unto the same.

And this did not happen by chance: it is all the work of Love, through the agency of music, that 'this goodly architecture wrought', as indeed did Amphion who with his charming lyre made 'the stones conspire/The ruins of a city to repair'. Penelope is being won over. Antinous tells her that the 'trembling lights numberless' of the stars:

> all move and in a dance express
> The great long year that doth contain no less
> Than three score hundreds of those years in all
> Which the sun makes with his course natural.

And this is again Plato, in his doctrine of the Great Year,—the
cycle in which the heavenly bodies go through all their possible
courses and return to their original positions relative to each
other.[34] This leads Davies to a characterization of each of the
planets (sts. 36–42). He firmly rejects the Copernican theory
(st. 51); 'Only the earth doth stand forever still', and yet we dance
on it. Thus, like Du Bartas, Davies brings in elements from the
Renaissance book of knowledge, giving them unity by subordi-
nating them to his dominant metaphor of the dance: he mentions
the seven motions in nature, metre in verse, Orpheus, the dance
of the Three Graces, Tiresias dancing as man and woman, the
dance forward of troops in war, and so on, in considerable
profusion, till Antinous' speech concludes:

> Lo! this is dancing's true nobility,
> Dancing, the child of Music and of Love;
> Dancing itself, both love and harmony,
> Where all agree and all in order move;
> Dancing, the art that all arts do approve;
> The fair character of the world's consent,
> The heaven's true figure, and the earth's ornament.

Sir Thomas Browne, as we might expect, manages to turn the most
orthodox of doctrines concerning world harmony to his own
personal uses. Like Shakespeare in *The Merchant of Venice*, he
admits the old objection to Pythagoras' doctrine that we cannot
actually hear the music of the spheres; yet

> there is a music wherever there is a harmony, order or
> proportion: and thus far we may maintain the music of
> the Sphears; for those well-ordered motions and regular
> paces, though they give no sound unto the ear, yet to the
> understanding they strike a note most full of harmony.
> Whosoever is harmonically composed delights in a
> harmony: which makes me much mistrust the symmetry
> of those heads which declaim against all Church-Musick.

And as we saw, even 'vulgar and Tavern-Musick' made Browne think of the 'First Composer'. His belief that men's souls may be at least 'harmonicall' gives him the metaphor he needs for the effects of his own conversation, in which he quite naturally keeps up as well the astronomical symbolism.

> For my conversation, it is like the Sun's with all men, and with a friendly aspect to good and bad. Methinks there is no man bad, and the worst, best; that is while they are kept within the circle of those qualities wherein they are good: there is no man's mind of such discordant and jarring a temper, to which a tuneable disposition may not strike a harmony.

The charm of Sir Thomas's thought, here as elsewhere, is that he manages to weld quite esoteric thoughts into prose which carries them with ease as readily intelligible metaphors. Thus in reading him one often has the impression of an elaborate counterpoint of ideas; nowhere more so than in his *Garden of Cyrus* (1658), in which 'The Quincunciall Lozenge, or Network Plantations of the Ancients, are Artificially, Naturally, Mystically considered'. His euhemeristic interpretations of Greek mythology make a charmingly fanciful reconciliation of the Greek and Biblical traditions: 'That *Vulcan* gave arrows unto *Apollo* and *Diana* the fourth day after their Nativity according to Gentile theology, may passe for no blinde apprehension of the Creation of the Sunne and Moon, in the work of the fourth day'.

He treats numerological thought as being on the highest level throughout this work. Alluding to the conception of two as the first feminine and three as the first masculine number, he tells us of the 'fantasticall Quincunx in *Plato* of the first hermaphrodite or double man, united at the Loynes, which Jupiter after divided'. But the most elevated chapter is of course the fifth, in which the quincunx is 'mystically considered'. He tries to avoid Pythagorean speculation, but cannot resist it:

> To enlarge this contemplation unto all the mysteries, and secrets, accommodable unto this number, were inexcusable Pythagorisme, yet cannot omit the ancient conceit of five surnamed the number of justness, as justly dividing between the digits, and hanging in the centre of

Nine described by square numeration, which angularly divided will make the decussated number.

The figure Browne has in mind is this one:

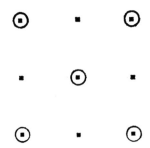

But this is a rather acrobatic way of trying to prove the digits of five to be fairly divided. Perhaps two numerological associations of justice are being confused here. Five was associated with justice because of the containment of the Law within the Pentateuch. More commonly, the number of justice was four or eight, on the old Pythagorean grounds of fair division or reciprocity. But Browne's attempt to make five 'justly divide' the digits in a square is certainly ingenious.

Five was also very importantly the number of marriage.

> Antiquity named this the Conjugall or wedding number, and made it the Embleme of the most remarkable conjunction . . . (This may) afford no improbable reason why *Plato* admitted his nuptial guests by fives, in the kindred of the married couple.

He alludes here to Plato, *Laws*, 6.

George Chapman takes up these hints from Plato in the numerologically significant fifth sestiad of his continuation of Marlowe's *Hero and Leander* (1598).[35] In this beautiful lyric epithalamion, Hero vicariously celebrates her love for Leander by solemnizing the marriage of two betrothed lovers, Almane and Mya. The 'tale of Teras' within this sestiad celebrates the love and marriage of Hymen and Eucharis. 'Gold lockt' Hymen goes to the church, preceded in due Platonic order by 'five lovely children deckt with ornament/Of her sweet colours'. This 'od disparent number' was chosen by them:

To show the union married loves should use,
Since in two equal parts it will not sever,
But in the midst holds one to rejoyne it ever,
As common to both parts: men therefore deeme,
That equal number Gods do not esteeme.
Being authors of sweet peace and unitie,
But pleasing to th' infernall Empire,
Under whose ensignes Wars and Discords fight,
Since an even number you may disunite
In two parts equall, nought in middle left,
To reunite each part from other reft:
And five they hold in most especiall prise,
Since t'is the first od number that doth rise
From the two formost numbers unitie
That od and even are; which are two, and three,
For one no number is: but thence doth flow
The powerfull race of number.[36]

Two was supposed to be an evil number partly because God
failed to say that it was good on the second day of creation; and
we saw that although Agrippa calls two the number of marriage
because there are two sexes, he also believed that the number
'doth cause apparitions of Ghosts, and fearfull goblins', presumably denizens of that infernal empire to which Chapman refers.

Browne in his turn develops the Platonic idea of processions of
five, as Chapman does, when he tells us that a 'sharper mystery'
might be implied in the number of the five wise and foolish virgins
who were to come forth to meet the bridegroom, and also that the
Romans 'admitted but five Torches in their Nuptiall solemnities'.

The climax of Browne's fifth chapter comes however in the
association of the quincunx with the Deity. Having explained to
us the technique of Gematria, Browne uses it to explain numerologically the foundation of Cusa's idea, found also in Plotinus and
the Hermetica, that God is the 'sphaera intelligibilis'. For five is a
circular number which when multiplied by itself 'will return into
its own denomination, and bring up the reare of the account'.
The argument is clinched for him when he reminds us that five
is the number of the name of God, which in gematria consists of
letters denoting the spherical numbers, ten, five and six: this
'Emphatically sets forth the Notion of *Trismegistus*, and that

intelligible Sphere, which is the Nature of God'. In view of this it is surprising that he distrusts Biblical numerology as perhaps making the Scriptures 'unjustly laden with mystical expositions'—but he still cannot resist citing a number of examples, and asking:

> why the radicall Letters in the Pentateuch, should equall the number of the Souldiery of the Tribes; Why our Saviour in the wilderness fed five thousand persons with five Barley Loaves, and again, but four thousand with no less than seven of Wheat? Why *Joseph* designed five changes of Rayment unto *Benjamin* and *David* took just five pebbles out of the Brook against the Pagan Champion? We leave it unto Arithmeticall Divinity, and Theologicall explanation.

The answers can indeed be found, in Bongo and other writers discussed above. For example, although David took five 'limpidissimos lapides' from the brook, symbolizing the law of the Pentateuch: 'sed uno spurium Goliath Philistaeum imprudenter exercitum dei viventis exprobrantem concussit, prostratumque occidit: quia in uno praecepto charitatis perficitur lex'.[37]

Browne has many more peculiar questions to ask about the number five, and as he tells us 'A large field is left unto sharper discerners to enlarge upon this order, . . . to erect generalities, disclose unobserved proprieties, not only in the vegetable shop, but the whole volume of nature'. And this is very much what we find in Agrippa and Giorgio! But Sir Thomas concludes his meditation on sleep, within which, in a beautiful and justly famous passage, he rises to the Platonic First Cause of All, dwelling in his numerologically ordered city of the Jerusalem of Apocalypse:

> Night which Pagan Theology could make the daughter of Chaos, affords no advantage to the description of order: Although no lower than that Masse can we derive its genealogy. All things began in order, so shall they end, and so shall they begin again: according to the ordainer of order and mystical Mathematics of the City of Heaven.

The theme of the moral effects of music is one which is very widely discussed in our period.[38] Music's angelic power, symbolized in the legends of David and Saul, and the Platonic idea of the tuneable soul, were the main topics. George Herbert's poetry is thus full of musical imagery, for example in *The Temper (I)*, where 'temper' carries the notion of tempering or tuning:

> Yet take Thy way: for sure Thy way is best:
> Stretch or contract me, Thy poore debter;
> This is but tuning of my breast,
> To make the musick better.

And John Donne, in his 'Hymne to God my God, in my sicknesse':

> Since I am comming to that Holy roome,
> Where, with thy Quire of Saints for ever more,
> I shall be made thy Musique; as I come
> I tune the Instrument here at the dore,
> And what I must doe then think here before.

These ideas of the tuning of the soul stem not only from the *Timaeus*, but also from the *Republic* (IV, 442–4) and *Phaedo* (86–94). Further, the modes of music were also held to have differing types of moral effect, for example the Doric mode was held by Aristotle (*Politics*, VIII, 7) to have a good ethical effect, and was fit to be taught to the young. Plato allows also the retention of the Phrygian mode (*Republic*, III, 398–400), rejecting the Mixed Lydian and Hyperlydian, as leading to drunkenness, effeminacy and idleness, and the Ionian and Lydian as 'lax', thus not usable in training men for war. The Phrygian and Dorian are retained, the one as violent, the other tranquil, thus suitable to imitate the tones of men in adversity and in prosperity. These views are alluded to in Marvell's poem on *The First Anniversary of the Government Under Oliver Cromwell*: in which Cromwell is 'identified with the Sun, and rises to the skies, where he learns the music of cosmic order, the music of the spheres, which is an order which he will transmit to the microcosm below, imposing thereon the political form of universal harmony'.[39] Cromwell's creation of order in England through his Instrument of Government of 1653 is thus compared to Amphion's building of the Walls of Thebes by the music of his lute, when:

> The listning Structures he with Wonder ey'd,
> And still new Stopps to various Time apply'd:
> Now through the Strings a Martial rage he throws,

And joyning straight the *Theban* Tow'r arose;
Then as he Strokes them with a touch more sweet,
The flocking Marbles in a Palace meet;
But for he most the graver Notes did try,
Therefore the Temples rear'd their Columns high:
Thus, ere he ceas'd his sacred Lute creates
Th' harmonious City of the seven Gates. (57–66)

The modes Amphion used thus being the Phrygian one of 'martial rage', the 'touch more sweet' of the Hyperlidian, and the 'grave notes' of the Dorian.

Not surprisingly, Cowley's *Davideis* (1656) develops similar themes, along with those of the *harmonia mundi*, in which he makes a close connection between the writing of poetry and creation. This is significant for us, in view of what we shall have to say about poetry which is numerologically structured. Unlike Milton and Dryden, who also are very much concerned with these ideas, Cowley cannot, as Hollander remarks, 'carry off an excited rendering of a musical composition-world creation conceit without having the seams of his learning show'.[40] Yet certain passages in his poem are interesting precisely because their leading ideas do have such strong overtones of their history. Especially significant are the allusions to numerological composition in these lines:

As first a various unformed Hint we find
Rise in some God-like Poets fertile Mind,
Till all the parts and words their places take
And with just marches verse and music make;
Such was Gods Poem, this Worlds new essay;
So wild and rude in its first draught it lay;
Th' ungoverned parts no Correspondence knew,
And artless war from thwarting Motions grew;
Till they to Number and fixt Rules were brought
By the Eternal Mind's Poetique Thought.
Water and Air he for the Tenor chose,
Earth made the Base, the Treble flame arose;
To th' active Moon a quick brisk stroke he gave,
To Saturns string a touch more soft and grave.
The motions Strait, and Round, and Swift, and Slow,
And Short and Long, were mixt and woven so,

Did in such awfull Figures smoothly fall,
As made this decent measured Dance of All.[41]

(The notion of the harmony of the elements has been remarked
upon above; the moon of course receives a 'quick brisk stroke'
since its orbit takes a mere 28 days, whereas Saturn's string
receives 'a touch more soft and grave' since its orbit takes 29 years.)
Cowley's note on this passage makes even more explicit the relationship between the concepts of mathematical creation and of
poetry:

> the *Scripture* witnesses, that the World was made in
> *Number*, *Weight*, and *Measure*; which are all qualities of
> a good *Poem*. This order and proportion of things is the
> true *Musick* of the world. . . .

Thus we are led to infer that the connections between music and
poetry are not simply a matter of the metaphorical content of
literary works. A connection was made between the two, which
embodies an assumption that may well have been in the minds of
those writers who gave their works a numerological structure.
Thus Puttenham precedes Cowley in remarking in his *Observations*
(1596) that 'the world is made by symmetry and proportion, and
is in that respect compared to music, and music to poetry'. This
remark only has point if Puttenham believed, as Cowley did, that
poetry can *share* in the musical proportioning of the *harmonia
mundi*. This very strong claim stretches right back over the
Renaissance period, for Ficino, having told us that through music
the soul can ally itself to the harmony of the universe, goes on
to say:

> But poetry is superior to music, since through the words
> it speaks not only to the ear but also directly to the mind.
> Therefore its origin is not in the harmony of the spheres,
> but rather in the music of the divine mind itself, and
> through its effect it can lead the listener directly to God
> Himself.[42]

3 Numerological Composition

These attempts to make poetry correspond to divine creation did
not remain on the level of mere metaphysical aspiration: poets

set out deliberately and very practically to structure poems so that they had a hidden meaning on the numerological-allegorical level, in accordance with the Neo-Platonic view of poetry, that it could reveal the structure of reality. It is only in recent years, however, that critics have begun to discover the latent meaning of these poems with a 'hidden sense'. In this section I shall analyse as examples their work on four numerological poems: Spenser's *Epithalamion*, Shakespeare's *Venus and Adonis*, Milton's *Ode on the Morning of Christ's Nativity* and Dryden's *Song for Saint Cecilia's Day*.

It will become apparent as I do this that the critic aware of the numerological tradition, has to be able to master a quite new technique of critical analysis, under conditions of some difficulty. Perhaps the chief one is the secrecy and esotericism of allegory by numbers. The writers leave us clues, as I shall try to show. But they are never explicit, and no major Renaissance writer has left us a plan or sketch of a numerological poem. This does not mean that numerological ideas were not current: perhaps they were so much accepted among learned persons that they did not need to be made too obvious. Certainly the rather casual discussion by Puttenham, and the broad satire of Jonson, tend to suggest that numerological ideas were in fact quite well known. Nevertheless those who wrote numerological poetry seem to have kept a truly Pythagorean silence about their specific methods. Henry More, for example, one of the leaders of the Cambridge Platonists, was author of many works in which the theological and philosophical implications of numbers are discussed, as in his *Conjectura Cabbalistica* (1653), and his *Visionis Ezekielis Expositio* (1677). He also wrote epics which were numerologically structured: yet he does not tell us what the meanings of the numbers controlling the structure of his own poems are.[43]

Nevertheless a number of successes have been achieved in this relatively new field of criticism. One of the most substantial, to which I have frequently referred, is Alastair Fowler's study of the *Faerie Queene, Spenser and the Numbers of Time*. He demonstrates that the poem:

> is in fact an astonishingly complex web of interlocking numerical patterns of many different kinds. We find numerological patterns in line-, stanza-, canto-, and book-totals; in the location of these units; and even in

the numbers of characters mentioned in each episode. Pythagorean number symbolism, astronomical number symbolism based on orbital period figures and on Ptolemaic star catalogue totals, medieval theological number symbolism: all these strands, and more besides, are worked together into what—in this respect at least— must be one of the most intricate poetic textures ever devised.[44]

We are thus given an indication of the vast number of things the critic has to be on the look out for in investigation of a number-symbolic poem. But it is very important to emphasize right at the beginning that the structure *must* have an intelligible and apt meaning relationship to the *content* of the poem. The semantics of the numbers involved must be in a reciprocal relationship with what we read in the first place. Only in this way, in default of any external evidence, can a numerical interpretation of the text be supported. Thus number symbolism 'gets into' poetry in two ways; either as aspects of the structure of the work, or as substantive symbols within it, such as we saw in Chapman's *Hero and Leander*. We must be on the alert for this sort of thing when we find contexts in which cosmology, music, astronomy, astrology, Biblical stories containing numbers, references to creation, and so on, are part of the subject-matter.

In investigating these literary texts we will often find larger numbers than those discussed so far. Some of them, like 300 as the number of the cross (the number of lines in Chapman's *Hymne to Our Sauior on the Crosse* (1612)), or 888, the gematric number of the name of Jesus, have a symbolism in their own right, as it were, as of course do the larger astronomical numbers (the most obvious being 365 as the number of a year). But most of these larger numbers are symbolic by virtue of being broken down by factorization. For example the Lady in Milton's *Comus* makes a speech in defence of Chastity of 60 lines long; Miss Røstvig holds this speech to symbolize the perfect fulfilment of the law, since it is made up of ten, the number of the decalogue, times six, the number of perfection. Of course this interpretation can only be effected in the context of the other number-symbolic devices demonstrated by Miss Røstvig: the critic must always ask himself whether the number could have occurred by chance. Conversely, the best external method of verification of a number-symbolic interpretation is to show by mathematical demonstration, as Dr Fowler frequently does, how very large the odds are against a particular numerical configuration having occurred by chance. Of course the example cited from *Comus* is a very simple one, like the fifty-nine lines of Faustus's last speech, which symbolizes the passing of his last hour on earth, or the concluding compass image of Donne's *A Valediction forbidding mourning*, about the two souls of the lovers:

> If they be two, they are two so
>   As stiff twin compasses are two,
> Thy soul the fixt foot, makes no show
> To move, but doth, if the 'other doe.
>
> And though it in the center sit,
>   Yet when the other far doth rome,
> It leans, and harkens after it,
>   It grows erect, as that comes home.
>
> So wilt thou be to mee, who must
>   Like th' other foot, obliquely runne;
> Thy firmness makes my circle just,
>   And makes me end, where I begunne.

These famous last verses can in fact be interpreted as describing the completion of the circle; as they bring the poem to its full complement of 36 lines, symbolizing the 360 degrees of a circle.[45]

Numerological criticism is at present very much an ongoing concern. In what follows I should like to give the reader a limited indication of its possibilities, by presenting, I am afraid often in much reduced form, the findings of the critics as they affect the four poems first mentioned.

The pioneering study in the field of Renaissance poetry was that by Kent Hieatt, of Spenser's *Epithalamion* (1575).[46] This case is particularly interesting, partly because it concerns a poem which has been the property of even unscholarly readers for so long, who yet failed to notice a symbolism in it which is in its essentials unesoteric. In demonstrating its numerological plan we will in fact need to appeal to nothing more than common knowledge. Hieatt's argument is also interesting, because it slowly builds up an amount and character of evidence that rules out any possibility of coincidence, as so much numerological exegesis has to do, if it is to be convincing. It is also of aesthetic significance, in that it instructs us in a way to read the poem, to structure it in our own experience. It very ingeniously enforces a parallel between time-taken-in-reading and time comprehended within the action of the poem. Hieatt's book itself must be consulted if one wishes to savour the excitement of his discovery and his full and complex argument. I can only indicate here his main findings, as indicating a type of numerological approach to a text.

Hieatt was faced with the facts that the stanza and line lengths of the poem seem to vary in an unconventional way. He thus had to develop an hypothesis to explain these apparently awkward features of the poem; for they were clearly intended. He was able to show that the stanza totals within the poem symbolized the lengths of day and night on a Midsummer's Day (which was the day of the marriage): for up to stanza seventeen the refrain to each stanza is in varying ways positive (e.g. 'To which the woods shall answer and theyr eccho ring'). After this point they are in varying ways negative (e.g. 'The woods no more shall answere, nor your eccho ring'). Now contemporary sources which were quite commonly known, such as Sacrobosco's *De Sphaera* or the *Kalender of Shepherdes* would have told Spenser and his readers, that the proportion of day to night on Midsummer's Day in a northern latitude is 16¼ hours of day to 7¾ hours of night. (This fact is also important in Shakespeare's *Venus and Adonis*, as we shall see.) Spenser actually marks the fall of night quite carefully in line 300 of his poem, at the end of the first of the four groups of long lines in the seventeenth stanza. Thus the poem is divided to symbolize exactly the proportion of day to night.

The hypothesis that the long lines of the poem symbolize the duration of time is strengthened even further once one notices that their total for the poem is 365, the number of days in a year. But yet another astronomical fact can be seen to be symbolized in the poem. The sun in its apparent daily movement through the zodiac of the fixed stars always 'falls back' by one degree in each twenty-four hours (these are symbolized by twelve matching pairs of stanzas in the poem which are matched in content, sc. 1–12 with 13–24). Thus the sun travels slowly backwards through the signs of the Zodiac. While the starry sphere has apparently rotated through 360 degrees each day round the earth, the sun will have passed through only 359 degrees. This aspect of the sun's daily movement is in fact alluded to in lines 267–9:

> Declining daily by degrees,
> He somewhat loseth of his heat and light.

Now, if we except the envoy to the poem of six lines, we find that Spenser ostensibly ends his poem about the day of his marriage in the 359th long line. Thus in Hieatt's words:

> the envoy, adding six more lines, expresses symbolically what this daily incompleteness of the sun entails: the creation of the measure of the solar year of 365 days, symbolized by the 365 long lines of the poem including its tornata.[47]

This may simply seem to be an ingenious description of a process of line-counting: but, as is essential if the interpretation is to be valid, the structural symbolism can be shown to be appropriate to the content of the poem. For the envoy reads:

> Song made in lieu of many ornaments,
> With which my love should duly have been dect,
> Which cutting off through hasty accidents,
> Ye would not stay your dew time to expect,
> But promist both to recompens,
> Be unto her a goodly ornament,
> And for short time an endless moniment.

Thus Hieatt demonstrates the vital content-structure relationship by pointing out that the song is incomplete and 'born before its due time' at the end of the twenty-third stanza, before the tornata, when it is only 359 lines long, just as the 359 degrees orbit of the sun is incomplete:

> yet this symbolic insufficiency of the song celebrating a day contains the promise of a recompense in and through the *tornata* which the ostensible insufficiency of the song itself calls forth, just as the sun contains the promise of the year—the perfect cyclical order by which, as Spenser has it in the Mutability Cantos, we, and the whole universe of time and space, exist through short time.[48]

Hieatt tells us a great deal more than I have been able to

indicate here about the number-symbolic features of this magnificent poem. In his fourth chapter, for example, he goes on to explain in similar fashion the symbolism of the short lines in the poem. Thus *Epithalamion* can be seen to be a great achievement of the poetic of correspondence and cosmic affinity, which I described above. For the poem is an extended analogy between the cycles of the seasons as they repeat themselves, and the continuance of life through human procreation, which is duly and properly celebrated in this marriage song.

The very same structural devices, of the proportions of day and night on Midsummer's Day, and of the 'falling short' by one degree in astronomical processes, were found by Alastair Fowler and the present writer in Shakespeare's *Venus and Adonis*.[49] The epigraph to this poem hints at the occultism associated with numerology:

> Vilia miretur vulgus: mihi flavus Apollo
> Pocula Castalia plena ministret aqua.

('Let the vulgar throng admire worthless things: but to me may the golden-haired Apollo supply cups filled at the Castalian stream', *Amores*, I, xv.)

The myth of Venus and Adonis is treated in this poem as it traditionally was, as having a seasonal temporal import. Under this interpretation Adonis, symbolizing the sun, parts from Venus, enacting the sun's entry into the lower or nocturnal hemisphere, marking the change from summer to winter. He is slain by the boar, which according to Sandys' commentary on Ovid, is the 'image of winter'.

Shakespeare keeps to this temporal interpretation of the myth, carefully noting the occurrence of mid-day and of sunset on the first day of the poem's action, and of sunrise on the second day (lines 1–3, 177–8, 529–30 and 856). Taking the total number of lines for 24 hours as 1032, and the modulus for one hour to be 43 lines, we find that the durations of the first day and night of the poem are approximately sixteen hours, twenty-five minutes for day, and seven hours thirty-five minutes for night. These figures are commensurable with those for a solstitial Midsummer's Day in a northern latitude. The number 1032 as a full day occurs again—for as Adonis dies in stanza 172, his life in the poem is in fact 1032 lines in duration. We can thus say that he is alive for twenty-four hours, which is understandable in view of his identification with the sun. We thus see that the 'internal' character of the symbolism such as we found it in Spenser's poem is preserved, but that Shakespeare's scheme is more hidden and complex, calling for a mathematical argument in parallel with the narrative of the poem.

Thus when Venus, separated from Adonis, sings her 'heavy anthem':

> Her song was tedious, and outwore the night,
> For lovers hours are long, though seeming short.

This is because the temporal nocturnal hours do in fact seem short in summer. Further, the numbers 353 and 326, which denote the semidiurnal and nocturnal periods in terms of line totals, are both curiously 'one short' of the lengths in days of the lunar synodic and sidereal years respectively. (The lunar synodic year is the number of days the moon takes to return to the same apparent position with respect to the zodiac; while the lunar sidereal year is twelve times the period from new moon to new moon.) There is another falling short too, for the number of stanzas from mid-day to sunset is fifty-nine—one short of the sixty minutes of the hour. 'Wasted in time-beguiling sport', a summer's day seems literally 'an hour but short', even if it is in fact the longest possible day. These failures to complete an expected measure are obviously to be related to the turning point of the poem's plot. For the latter is also a failure to reach fulfilment; Venus, unable to seduce Adonis, finds that even when she is in 'the very lists of love' she has to 'clip Elizium and to lack her joy'. And the frustration of Venus occurs at the very centre of the poem, which is often numerologically significant; two further examples will be cited later.

So far the keys to the hidden sense of this poem have lain in its correct division into, and, as for *Epithalamion*, subsequent correlation with, easily available astronomical facts. (The great interest in these in our period needs no further emphasis.) But in fact this poem also refers numerologically within itself. For we were also puzzled by Venus's strange prediction of the duration of the kisses given in the poem:

> And yet not cloy thy lips with loath'd satiety,
> But rather famish them amid their plenty,
> Making them red, and pale, with fresh variety:
> Ten kisses short as one, one long as twenty.
> A summer's day will seem an hour but short,
> Being wasted in such time-beguiling sport.

In fact the line 'ten kisses short as one, one long as twenty' literally expresses the ratio of their durations in the poem. The first ten kisses given by Venus to Adonis up to the end of the first ten stanzas, occupy the same space as the one kiss given by Adonis to Venus in stanza 90, which has taken ten stanzas to elicit. Here indeed is the 'numbring of kisses', of Cleveland's poem.

A third type of number symbolism which we tried to explain in this poem was concerned with the number twenty. It seemed to connote grief:

> Ay me! she cries, and twenty times, 'Woe, woe',
> And twenty echoes twenty times cry so.

This is in agreement with Bongo, who says 'numquam vicenarium adhibet, nisi ad res tristes, luctuosas, acerbas . . .'. But one would expect this number, in view of the character of the other number symbolism of the poem, to have a temporal import. The clue to the answer was given by the dedication to Southampton, who was exactly twenty years old in the year of the poem's first appearance, 1593. We then understood why the poem contained so many references to Adonis' age, why he should appeal to Venus, 'measure my strangeness with my unripe years', and why:

> Were beauty under twenty locks kept fast,
> Yet love breaks through, and picks them all at last.

This connection between Adonis and Southampton then helped us to explain the length of the poem, which is 20 times 60, or 1200 lines, a representation of twenty hours. This reinforces the theme of time's brevity. Southampton's twenty summers seem but twenty hours. With these facts in mind, we could go on to explain the number of kisses exchanged between Venus and Adonis in the poem. This depends on another astronomical fact which is alluded to in Davies's *Orchestra*, for in that poem we are told that:

> Venus the mother of that bastard love
> Which doth usurp the world's great marshal's name,
> Just with the sun her dainty feet doth move,
> And unto him doth all her gestures frame;
> Now after, now afore, the flattering dance
> With divers cunning passages doth err,
> Still him respecting that respects not her.

Here Davies both retails the theme of the myth that Shakespeare uses, and reminds us that the motion of the planet Venus in the sky appears as an oscillation from one side of the sun to the other. The complete period of the oscillation is about 1.6 years, of 584 days. In elongation east of the sun Venus is the evening star, and to the west it is the morning star. Now in view of the planetary functions of the main characters of Shakespeare's poem, we should expect their kisses to refer to the conjunctions between Venus and the sun. And in fact their closeness as they kiss is stressed—'In corporate then they seem, face grows to face'—'their lips together glued'. Moreover, the most elaborately described kiss, that begun in stanza 90, occurs at sunset, one of the two occasions when the two are seen in the sky together. Now the number of inferior conjunctions between the two planets, when Venus is the brighter of the two, occurs at such an interval that in the twenty years of Southampton's lifetime, a total of twelve occurred. That is the number of kisses exchanged in the poem.[50]

The two poems we have so far interpreted numerologically have been treated as structures of quite specific astronomical numbers, all interlocking. We can say with some degree of certainty that our interpretation is correct, as the separate numbers fall into place within the scheme. But in the poem we come to next, Milton's *Nativity Ode*, we are reliant upon the connotations of relatively few numbers, which are less specifically related to the content of the poem than are those in *Venus and Adonis*. Our treatment of the poem then becomes more of a true interpretation, subject to varying opinion, rather than an explanation of what is there. In discussing Miss Røstvig's interpretation I do not wish to imply that she is simply mistaken—her work in the whole field of numerology has been much too exact and perceptive for that, and the great majority of her findings seem to be certain. But I wish to discuss this particular poem to show how numerological interpretation may become a kind of allegory of a poem, a reading of it on the anagogical level.

The introduction to this poem consists of four seven-line stanzas (28 lines), and the following Hymn of 27 eight-line stanzas (216 lines). Miss Røstvig claims that 'in the introduction we are in the world of man, a world dominated by the constantly changing lunar and solar phases'.[51] Thus the introductory structure suggests time and mutability, with the 28-day phase of the moon, the seven-day week, and the four stanzas symbolizing the 'darksome house of mortal clay', the earth, made up of the four elements. Thus Milton asks himself:

> Hast thou no verse, no hymn or solemn strain
> To welcome him to this his new abode?

Miss Røstvig also points out that the number of metric syllables in each stanza is 72, which is the complete cycle of years attributed to man in the cycle from birth to death.

Thus for her the transition from the stanzas of seven lines to those of eight lines in the succeeding Hymn, symbolizes the movement from the world of time, 'the cosmic week of seven ages within which the history of fallen man is acted out', to the eighth age, of the reign of Christ. This doctrine of the separate ages is indeed a traditional one. For example, Clement, Victorinus and Basil all interpret the resurrection of Christ on the eighth day as symbolizing the eighth age, endless and timeless, when we shall enjoy our future glory. Thus the Hymn is completely dominated by numbers of timelessness and harmony, especially eight and twenty-seven. Indeed in the Hymn we are told that Cynthia (sc. the moon) knew:

> her part was don,
> And that her reign had here its last fulfilling;
> She knew such harmony alone
> Could hold all Heav'n and Earth in happier union.

As Miss Røstvig points out, Milton's direct exhortation to his muse, 'join thy voice unto the angel quire' suggests that the ratios or proportions which determine the angels' song will also control the structure of the Hymn. Thus the angels' 'ninefold harmony' is reflected in the triple division of the Hymn, into nine stanzas each, while the eight lines in each stanza symbolize the musical octave or diapason and also the eighth age of the world.

Up to this point I am in complete agreement with the interpretation I have outlined here: it seems entirely appropriate to the content and intention of the poem. But Miss Røstvig goes on to say:

> Milton's statement that 'Time will run back and fetch the age of gold' (line 135) may refer to the wider idea (also expressed by Giorgio) that since Christ rose on the eighth day, which is also the first day of the week, eight returns to unity. In other words, the eighth age of the reign of Christ will mark a return to the perfect diapason of the prelapsarian world, in which multiplicity is reconciled to unity, the res creata being one with God.

Here one may feel that allegorization of the text has gone beyond what is justified by its content. Certainly we stay within the terms of reference set by the number eight. But the chief difficulty here is that there seems to be nothing in the text, of which the interpretation can be taken to be a proper paraphrase or explication, though indeed the interpretation of eight as returning to unity is plausible. (For since in the story of creation God rested on the seventh day, at the end of which there was no evening, commentators took the eighth day as meaning a return to the original innocent state of creation, now made eternal.) But the impression is given of a number-symbolic meditation on the significance of Christ's nativity, which develops a little beyond what we have in the text. We have an allegory alongside the poem. The same criticisms seem to me to apply to Miss Røstvig's attempt to make the Hymn an allegory of creation, ingenious as it certainly is. For she goes on to compare the three groups of nine stanzas of the Hymn to the diapason and diapente of Giorgio's 27-pace nave for the church of San Francesco della Vigna. Thus, considering the poem as a structure reflecting world creation, in the same way as Giorgio's church does, she can say:

> if we consider 8 as part of the Platonic *Lambda* where 27 is at the other end of the scale, 8 symbolizes the passive matter out of which the hymn is created by means of the active principle of form symbolized by the cube of 3.

Now this is a brilliant suggestion as to what may go on in the mind of a poet inspired to create as God was supposed to have done in his creation. But there can be little evidence for this private act of intention, in default of a much clearer expression of it than we actually have in Milton's poem. The evidence for saying that God was thought to have 'geometrized constantly', and for saying that Milton is doing so as well in writing, fail to correspond to one another. It is in accord with this interpretation above that Miss Røstvig can say that the total line count for the Hymn of 216, can symbolize 'perfection kept steady in three dimensional security', for the poem is the multiple of the cubes of 8 and 27. But she also acknowledges a suggestion of Dr Fowler's, that 216 is the 'psychogonicos cubos' expressing the term in days of the seven-month child, and this seems more perfectly in accord with the theme of the poem.

The fourth interpretation of a number-symbolic poem that I wish to discuss is that by Douglas Brooks and Alastair Fowler, of Dryden's 'Song for St. Cecilia's Day' (1687).[52] We are irresistibly led to expect that this poem will be numerologically structured, as soon as we know that its themes are music and creation, and, what is more, creation considered as a form of music:

> As from the pow'r of Sacred Lays
>   The Spheres began to move,
> And sung the great Creator's praise
>   To all the blessed above. . . .

The inner stanzas of the poem deal with the effects of music on man; 'What Passion cannot MUSICK raise and quell!' Thus stanzas iii–vi describe the types of music affecting the four temperaments: choleric, melancholic, phlegmatic and sanguine, 'equivalents in man of the four concordant elements that separate from Chaos to form the macrocosm'. Brooks and Fowler go on to point out that these stanzas mention instruments which are iconographically appropriate to the passions—trumpet and drum for anger (st. iii) as confirmed by reference to Kircher's *Musurgia Universalis* (1650), and Mersenne's *Harmonie Universelle* (1636). In the latter source a reference to promptitude as an attribute of choler explains the verse's change to an anapaestic metre in this stanza. Similarly, we are told by them that the flute (st. iv) is peculiarly appropriate to the Lydian mode, assigned to melancholy, and the phlegmatic's affinity to sharp sounds corresponds to the 'Sharp VIOLINS' of st. v. Stanza vi comes as a climax, because traditionally the sanguine man had the best tempered constitution, the *complexio temperata*, in which he most resembled the sinless Adam. Hence the introduction in this stanza of the 'sacred ORGAN', the supreme instrument which contained within it all the modes, St Cecilia's own instrument.

Brooks and Fowler treat all this evidence, amply supported by references to Kircher and Mersenne, as leading us to expect a numerological structure for the poem. They refer us indeed to the passage from Cowley, and its note, quoted above, concerning the 'eternal Minds Poetique Thought'. They explain the repetition of the lines:

> From Harmony, from heav'nly Harmony
> This universal Frame began—

in the first stanza, as dividing the stanza into two groups of ten and five lines, expressing a diapason, or perfect consonance, and also as enclosing within the repetition an octave of eight lines. Thus the stanza conveys in formal terms also, the 'Diapason closing full in Man'. In enclosing these eight lines the poem enacts the creation's cyclic return to unison, already remarked upon with reference to Milton's *Nativity Ode*. What is more, the 'frame' leaves over three lines, this time expressing the ratio for the whole stanza of 12:3 or 4:1, i.e. the disdiapason or double octave—and further, the total number of lines is 15, the number of notes played if we run through two octaves on an instrument (for the tonic note would be sounded only three, not four, times).

The overall construction of the poem in eight stanzas reaffirms this initial theme of circular return, for the poem ends with the same rhyme as it begins with, and, as Brooks and Fowler point out, there are further correspondences of content between stanzas and within stanzas, where the echo in wording mimics the octave return. Even the number of instruments mentioned in the poem, ten, marks this return to unity or the monad, for as we know, in Pythagorean thought ten and its multiples can stand for unity. What is more, ten is a form of the tetraktys $(1 + 2 + 3 + 4 = 10)$ which as we have also seen, was believed to contain the intervals on which the harmony of the universe was based.

In considering the numerology of the line totals of the other stanzas, Brooks and Fowler come to the conclusion that the poem is based on an antithesis between the numbers seven and nine, in which the former is considered as corporeal and the latter spiritual, as it traditionally was, where seven is the number of the body, and of the world as a mutable entity, and nine is the number of the mind, the spheres, the angelic hierarchies, and of heaven itself. They develop this theme at some length with reference to the authorities. Thus they conclude that:

> there is a relation of line count numerology between two stanzas already shown to be paired in another way. Stanzas ii and vii (which are connected by the correspondence of Jubal's and Orpheus' lyres) have 9 and 7 lines respectively. Together, they compose a double diapason or harmony, which 'frames' or tempers the same four central stanzas (the passions) that it—in another sense—'frames' spatially. The pattern is completed by the creation of another double diapason, for the seven lines of stanza vii are succeeded by the nine lines of stanza viii. We are no doubt intended to hear this last double diapason as a response to the initial one announced in stanza i. The octave symbolism, it seems, is meant to convey much more than a diffuse sense of harmoniousness.

It is then pointed out that stanza ii, possessing a circular structure of its own, containing a seven-line narrative within two repeated lines, echoes the larger framing of the temperaments by Stanzas ii and vii. The two numbers involved here, seven and nine, also control the structure of the poem. Since seven and nine were corporal and spiritual in import respectively, they were thought to have power to determine the critical stages of human life. Thus there were two climacterics, 49 and 81 (7^2 and 9^2). But the most important, since it pertained to the spiritual and corporeal, was the median one, 63, i.e. seven times nine. This is alluded to in the line total for the poem, of 63.

Further, in view of the poem's theme of creation leading to the Last Judgment, the addition of an eighth italicized stanza chorus to the previous seven takes on significance as symbolizing the eighth age of eternity and regeneration, when

> The TRUMPET shall be heard on high,
> The Dead shall live, the Living die,
> And MUSICK shall untune the Sky.

Thus Dryden stresses the resurrection, which in the case of Christ was supposed to have taken place on the eighth day after the beginning of Holy Week, in this eighth and last stanza.

Perhaps the greatest challenge to numerological criticism, after Dr Fowler's work on the *Faerie Queene*, now comes from Milton. All the preconditions for number-symbolic practice seem to be present: for he is an immensely learned poet, a man who managed to 'syncretize' diverse intellectual traditions into their true element, poetry, in which the logical inconsistencies, which arise from trying to reconcile thinkers of actually diverse viewpoint, are dissolved in metaphors and analogies in their proper plane of discourse. We find in him the full richness of the Christian tradition along with classical mythology, Orphism, the cabbala, and Neo-Platonic theology. All these, as we know, had important numerological elements. St Augustine, St Basil, Epicurus, Lucretius, Hesiod, Ezekiel and Proclus are all present in *Paradise Lost*, helping Milton to fill out his vast scheme, in which all this apparently merely eclectic conglomeration of ideas is subordinated to the narrative of man's first disobedience. Since we know from the poetic tradition immediately preceding him that numerology was not simply the province of mystagogues and cranks but part of the equipment of major writers, and with Miss Røstvig's analysis of the *Nativity Ode* and *Comus* before us, we can expect Milton to use the allegorical resources of number symbolism in his major narrative works.

We have in *Paradise Lost*, too, just those features that lead to number symbolism; the projection of a complete universe, and a description of its creation; the attempted reconciliation of arts and sciences in Raphael's account of astronomy (which is descended from Du Bartas); and actors in the drama whose doings are of such universal significance that we should not be surprised to find that they have a further allegorical dimension. Indeed, as far as the matter of poetic creation is concerned,

Marvell, in his commendatory verses to the second edition of *Paradise Lost*, provides us with a very significant clue, one which, as we shall see, marks an important link between the numerological practice of both writers. For he tells us that:

> Thy verse, created like thy Theme sublime,
> In Number, Weight and Measure, needs not *Rime*.

We can in fact begin our discussion of *Paradise Lost* at the appropriate Pythagorean starting-point, the conception of the *harmonia mundi*. Milton defended this from the earliest point in his career: in his *De Sphaerarum Concentu*, composed as a public oration at the university, he attacks Aristotle's refutation of Pythagoras, and in *Arcades* he states clearly his belief in harmonic proportions throughout the world, alluding to the music of the spheres, and the Spindle of Necessity in Plato's myth of Er.

> But els in deep of night when drowsiness
> Hath lockt up mortal sense, then listen I
> To the celestial *Sirens* harmony,
> That sit upon the nine enfolded Sphears,
> And sing to those that holds the vital shears,
> And turn the Adamantine spindle round,
> On which the fate of Gods and men is wound.
> Such sweet compulsion doth in Musick ly,
> To lull the daughters of *Necessity*,
> And keep unsteddy Nature to her law,
> And the low world in measur'd motion draw
> After the heavenly tune, which none can hear
> Of human mould with gross unpurgèd ear. (61–73)

In his *At a Solemn Music* he brings this pagan theme into a Christian context, when he tells us that at the fall:

> Disproportioned Sin
> Jarred against nature's chime, and with harsh din
> Broke the fair music that all creatures made.

And in *Paradise Lost* we find that the Fall 'distempers' the breast of Adam, now prey to 'high Passions', and the Father speaks of the

> dissolution wrought by Sin, that first
> Distempered all things, and of incorrupt corrupted.
> (IX, 1131 and XI, 55–57)

Not only this: but the 'fair music' of the heavens is broken too; for the profound astronomical changes at the Fall (X 648 ff) disrupt the 'Mystic dance, not without song', of the planets (V, 178). Before the Fall, even the 'Vulgar Constellations thick' from the 'Lordly eye' of the sun 'keep distance due':

> they as they move
> Thir Starry dance in numbers that compute
> Days, months, and years, towards his all-chearing Lamp
> Turn swift thir various motions. . . .
>
> (III, 579–82)

The angels who constantly praise God (III, 344 ff.) are compared, as they dance, to the stars, and God takes pleasure in the harmonies of his own created world:

> That day, as other solem days, they spent
> In song and dance about the sacred Hill,
> Mystical dance, which yonder starrie Spheare
> Of Planets and of fixt in all her Wheeles
> Resembles nearest, mazes intricate,
> Eccentric, intervolv'd, yet regular
> Then most, when most irregular they seem:
> And in thir motions harmonie Divine
> So smooths her charming tones, that Gods own ear
> List'ns delighted.
>
> (V, 618–27)

These quotations tend to show, I think, that Milton took the idea of the *harmonia mundi* quite seriously. Ludvig Spaeth in fact comes to the conclusion that:

> Milton's natural love of the orderly and the mathematical inspired in him a more than usual interest in the so-called 'measurable music'. The Pythagorean system of numbers, the necessary relationships of concord and discord, the mysteries of 'proportion' in pitch and rhythm, exercised upon him a peculiar fascination which is reflected in numerous allusions throughout his works. He regards number and measure as essential in music because they give it objective reality and permanence. Without this mathematical foundation music, as a science or even as a

scientific art, could not exist. And since number and measure are universal music is therefore an essential and inherent part of the universe.[53]

This musico-mathematical conception so permeates Milton's thinking that, as we shall see, he often gives us a musical clue to the number-symbolic passages in *Paradise Lost*.

He is also quite clear about the uses of the musical modes: the fallen angels in Hell move:

> In perfect *Phalanx* to the *Dorian* mood
> Of Flutes and soft Recorders; such as rais'd
> To highth of noblest temper Hero's old
> Arming to Battel, and in stead of rage
> Deliberat valour breath'd, firm and unmov'd
> With dread of death to flight or foul retreat,
> Nor wanting power to mitigate and swage
> With solemn touches, troubl'd thoughts, and chase
> Anguish and doubt and fear and sorrow and pain
> From mortal or immortal minds.
>
> (I, 550–9)

The Dorian mood here is very appropriate to 'imitate the tones of men in adversity', as we saw from Plato: who wanted 'to have one (mode) warlike, which will sound the word or note which a brave man utters in the hour of danger, and stern resolve, or when his cause is failing, and he is going to wounds or death or is overtaken by some other evil, and at every such crisis meets fortune with calmness and endurance'.

However, in the actual process of Creation, there seem to be very few Platonic elements: the model here seems to be a Lucretian atomism, as Curry's study has shown.[54] In Chaos:

> hot, cold, moist, and dry, four Champions fierce
> Strive here for Maistrie, and to battle bring
> Thir embryon Atoms. . . .
>
> (II, 898 ff.)

Nevertheless, Satan rides up through Chaos in the Platonic form of a pyramid of fire (II, 1013) and God seems at one point to be described in Neo-Platonic style as the Supreme Monad, generator of all Number, for Adam addresses God, saying:

> No need that thou
> Shouldst propagate, already infinite;
> And through all numbers absolute, though One
>
> (VIII, 419–21)

and when he goes on to speak of the human need for propagation he seems to allude to the divisive, imperfect qualities of the number two, for:

> Man by number is to manifest
> His single imperfection, and beget
> Like of his like, his Image multipli'd,
> In unitie defective, which requires
> Collateral love, and deerest amitie.

Raphael's account of creation (VII, 216 ff.) and his fence-sitting description of the Ptolemaic and Copernican systems in Book VIII, 123 ff., seem to owe little to numerological ideas, being indebted to the Biblical and text-book accounts respectively.

It is when we come to consider Milton's epic as a literary structure, that numerological elements really come into prominence. Miss Røstvig has shown very penetratingly that Milton used speech-line totals in *Comus* with symbolic properties. Certain key speeches there embody numbers in keeping with their contents; indeed we are told that some of them are supposed to be magical in effect, 'words set off by some adjuring power', which Comus fears in the Lady.

Thus Comus's first speech, which is addressed to the created physical universe, dedicated to the sphere of mutability, contains fifty-two lines, symbolizing the weeks of the year. The second part of this speech contains twenty-five lines, the square of five, here the number of the senses. Bongo, as Miss Røstvig points out, makes twenty-five the number of 'homines sensuales, idolatras, ac consummatum illorum malitiam atque induratem obstinationem', which is a good description of Comus, whose

> Well plac't words of glozing courtesie
> Baited with reasons not unplausible
> Wind me into the easie-hearted man,
> And hug him into snares.

Satan, as we shall see, has the same power, when he his 'proem tunes' before Eve. Comus's further defences of pleasure (665–689 and 706–755) are twenty-five and fifty lines long, and the same reasoning applies.

These speeches in *Comus*, and key speeches in *Paradise Lost*, thus manifest the

> secret power
> Of harmony in tones and numbers hit
> By voice or hand, in various measured verse,

which in *Paradise Regained* (IV, 254–6) Milton specifically tells us could be learnt at Athens, 'the eye of Greece', 'Mother of Arts/ And Eloquence'. And in *Paradise Lost* (II, 552 ff.) when the fallen angels sing:

> Thir Song was partial, but the harmony
> (What could it less when Spirits immortal sing?)
> Suspended Hell, and took with ravishment
> The thronging audience. In discourse more sweet
> (For Eloquence the Soul, Song charms the Sense,)
> Others apart sat on a Hill retir'd,
> In thoughts more elevate. . . .

This is a remarkable echo of the view of Ficino quoted earlier, when he tell us that poetry speaks directly to the human soul by participating in the harmony of the divine mind itself. Thus it is hardly without reason that Milton invokes the Holy Spirit to inspire him to 'feed on thoughts, that voluntarie move/Harmonious numbers' in his verse (III, 37).

My findings concerning number-symbolic speeches in *Paradise Lost* can only be tentative—the evidence depends as usual upon its cumulative character. The speeches I believe to be number-symbolic are, with the important exception of the speeches of Christ, either of praise or of evil intent.

Uriel's speech in praise of the creation (III, 694–735) takes 42 lines, that is, the number of days of creation, seven, times six, the number of perfection. As he tells Satan, who deceives him:

> thy desire which tends to know
> The works of God, thereby to glorifie
> The great Work-Maister, leads to no excess
> That reaches blame, but rather merits praise. . . .

and he goes on to describe how the Platonic Work-Maister or Demiurge (for 'Work-Maister' translates the Greek expression) ordered the elements and 'this Ethereal quintessence of Heav'n', and how the moon helps to mark night and day on earth. Raphael also seems to use the number of perfection in his speech on the senses (V, 404–33), which are possessed even by angels who also:

> contain
> Within them every lower facultie
> Of sense, wherby they hear, see, smell, touch, taste,
> Tasting concoct, digest, assimilate,
> And corporeal to incorporeal turn.

For this speech contains thirty lines, six, the number of perfection, times five, the number of the senses. The invocation 'Haile wedded love' (IV, 750–70) may well also be number-symbolic for this

> true sourse
> Of human ofspring, sole proprietie,
> In Paradise of all things common else

with its stress on the distinctively human, runs for 21 lines. And Bongo tells us that the number twenty-one signifies 'absolutionem humanae perfectionis, quae in firma summae Trinitatis fide, et Spiritus Sancti gratia praesertim consistit'.[55]

When Adam and Eve come to praise God, we are given a very strong clue that what they say will be number-symbolic, and a hint as to the character of the symbolism:

> for neither various stile
> Nor holy rapture wanted they to praise
> Thir Maker, in fit strains pronounc't or sung
> Unmeditated, such prompt eloquence
> Flowd from thir lips, in Prose or numerous Verse,
> More tuneable then needed Lute or Harp
> To add more sweetness. . . .

For in their subsequent speech (V, 153–208) we have yet again the number seven for creation, times the musical number eight.

> These are thy glorious works, Parent of good,
> Almightie, this thine universal Frame,
> Thus wondrous fair; thy self how wondrous then!

and the whole speech is permeated with musical imagery:

> Angels, for yee behold him, and with songs
> And choral symphonies, Day without Night,
> Circle his throne rejoycing . . .
> Thou Sun, of this great World both Eye and Soule,
> Acknowledge him thy Greater, sound his praise
> In thy eternal course. . . .
> And yee five other wandring Fires that move
> In mystic Dance not without Song, resound
> His praise, who out of Darkness call'd up Light.

They even invoke the 'Fountains and yee that warble' to 'tune his praise'. They also draw attention to the night-and-day symbolism of the number seven when they say that:

> if the night
> Have gatherd aught of evil or conceald,
> Disperse it, as now light dispells the dark.

This interpretation is further confirmed once we discover that in this speech there are sixteen separate invocations, and indeed, sixteen uses of the word 'yee'—two octaves for the two speakers.

The speeches of evil connotation in the poem which are number-symbolic are Eve's account of her dream which takes 66 lines (V, 28–93), which may be interpreted as the number of the Beast, and Satan's proem, which he 'tun'd' for the ear of Eve, which runs for seventeen lines (IX, 532–48) for which number Bongo has little good to say in his chapter on it.[56] According to Pristine Theology, he says, it has always been a detested and loathed number. He points out that in Roman numeral form it may spell VIXI—and Satan conquers Eve. He tells us also that it portends death, and referring to Genesis chapter 6 tells us that the number portends 'terrae motus, incendia, inundationes, multaque aliorum malorum genera'—all of which were consequences of the Fall.

Not only are there numerologically composed speeches scattered about the poem: they are also part of its very structure, as Quarnstrom has shown.[57]

He demonstrates that *Paradise Lost* and Benlowe's *Theophila* (1652) which latter poem his book is primarily concerned with, are both centrally constructed poems. He shows that in *Theophila* there is a central moral reversal in a verse paragraph about Christ of 23 stanzas, which is signalled as the centre of the poem by the insertion of an extra odd line.[58] He then points out that the 'focal paragraph' of *Paradise Lost*, that in which Christ ascends into his Chariot, runs from VI, 723 to 823, and is flanked on either side by 23-line speeches made by Christ. According to Bongo, the number 23 signifies divine judgment upon sinners, in accordance with *Exodus* and 1 *Corinthians* 10:8, where twenty-three thousand men are punished by God for idolatory and fornication. The number also has a contrary connotation as the sum of 3 and 20, of which 3 implies sincere Christian belief, and 20 the two-fold represented decalogue, thus comprising in Bongo's phrase, 'the fulfilment of man's salvation'. These symbolisms are appropriate to the content of these speeches of Christ in Book V and also to his speech of intercession in Book XI, lines 22–44 (not remarked upon by Quarnstrom).

Further, the sentence describing Christ's ascent into his chariot:

> Hee in Celestial Panoplie all armd
> Of radiant *Urim*, work divinely wrought,
> Ascended, at his right hand Victorie
> Sate Eagle-winged; beside him hung his Bow
> And Quiver with three-bolted Thunder stor'd,
> And from about him fierce Effusion rowld
> Of smoak and bickering flame, and sparkles dire;
> Attended with ten thousand thousand Saints,
> He onward came, farr off his coming shon,
> And twentie thousand (I thir number heard)
> Chariots of God, half on each hand were seen:
> Hee on the wings of Cherube rode sublime
> On the Crystallin Skie, in Saphir Thron'd,

lies exactly across the middle line of the whole epic. This is so both for the 1674 and 1667 editions of the poem. The numberings also apply equally to the two editions, for the speeches discussed above, and have thus been preserved across the changes made by Milton between the two editions.

There is a further confirmation of this interpretation of *Paradise Lost* as centrally planned, first pointed out to me by Alastair Fowler. We remember that Marvell commended Milton's poem as created 'In Number, Weight, and Measure', presumably indicating that he was aware of its numerological elements. Now in the very centre line of his own poem, the *First Anniversary* commented on above, Cromwell falls out of his carriage (as indeed he did when driving in Hyde Park on September 29 1649):

> Thou *Cromwell* falling, not a stupid Tree,
> Or Rock so savage, but it mourn'd for thee:
> And all about was heard a Panique groan,
> As if that Nature's self were overthrown.

This is not, as it may seem, mock heroic, but as the tone of the whole poem makes clear, simply rather grossly hyperbolic praise, such as we also found in *Appleton House*. And it parallels in a remarkable way the central incident in *Paradise Lost*.

Indeed I would suggest, though tentatively, that *Paradise Lost* in its twelve-book version is a symmetrical structure, with a 'double centre' in Books VI and VII which contain the two climaxes, of the Exaltation of the Son in the sixth book (the central episode on a line-count) and the creation of the heavens and of man in the seventh. About this centre the books correspond in other ways. The Satanic debate of I and II is balanced by that between Adam and Michael in XI and XII. Books III and X are also concerned with dialogues between God the Father and the Son, and also with Satan's journeys—in the first of these to Earth, and in the second back to Pandemonium. Books IV and IX are concerned with the relationship between Adam and Eve, before and after the Fall. At the centre lie Raphael's four books of exposition, concerning events outside the human time-scheme of the epic—the war in Heaven, the exaltation of the Son, and Creation.[59]

Notes

[1] John Donne, in his section 'Of Moses' in *Essays in Divinity* (Simpson, pp. 10–11). Even though he seems to have a low opinion of these writers as having 'many delicacies of honest and serviceable curiosity, and harmless recreation and entertainment', he yet gives an extended account of the symbolism of the number 70 in the Bible (Simpson, p. 57 ff.).

[2] *Architectural Principles in the Age of Humanism* (London, 1962), p. 23. On musical consonances in Gothic architecture, see Otto von Simson, *The Gothic Cathedral* (1956), pp. 21–58 et passim.

[3] Wittkower's discussion is in op. cit., p. 102 ff. The memorandum, from which I quote, is on p. 155 ff.

[4] Op. cit., p. 102.

[5] See Fowler, *Spenser and the Numbers of Time*, appendix I, p. 260 ff.

[6] *Sir Thomas Tresham and his Buildings*, Part II of the Reports and Papers of the Northamptonshire Antiquarian Society (1964–5), p. 15.

[7] Op. cit., p. 21.

[8] J. Alfred Gotch, *The Buildings of Sir Thomas Tresham*, Northamptonshire and London, 1883.

[9] Henry Wotton, *Elements of Architecture* (London, 1624), pp. 22–3.

[10] Op. cit., p. 12.

[11] Alberti, *De Re Aedificatoria*, chap. V, ed. of 1485, fol y iiiii v. Quoted by Wittkower, op. cit., p. 27, fn.

[12] Wotton, op. cit., pp. 53–5.

[13] On Dürer and his theory of proportion generally, see E. Panofsky, *Meaning in the Visual Arts* (New York, Garden City, 1955), ch. 2.

[14] Cf. Hilliard's *A Treatise concerning the Art of Limning*, ed. P. Norman, Walpole Society I (1912).

[15] *Satyre*, IV, 197–210.

[16] Entitled 'A Tracte containing the Artes of Curious Paintinge Carvinge and Buildynge, written first in Italian by Jo. Paul Lomatius of Milan'. The translation is dedicated to Thomas Bodley. A treatise on proportion in the arts, of far greater importance than Lomazzo's, was Luca Pacioli's *De Divina Proportione* (Venice, 1509). Pacioli was a disciple of Piero della Francesca, and his book is illustrated by Leonardo da Vinci.

[17] 'Mark Antony' in *Minor Poets of the Caroline Period*, ed. Saintsbury, III, 70.

[18] *Renaissance and Seventeenth Century Studies* (London, 1964), pp. 32–3, fn.

[19] For the relationship between seventeenth-century poetry and the 'new science', see esp. Marjorie Hope Nicolson, *The Breaking of the Circle* (1940), C. M. Coffin, *John Donne and the New Philosophy* (1938), and Kester Svendsen, *Milton and Science* (1956).

[20] F. R. Johnson, *Astronomical Thought in Renaissance England* (Baltimore, 1937), cf. esp. p. 3.

[21] *The Poetry of Meditation* (1962, rev. ed.), pp. 211–48.

[22] Cornford, *Plato's Cosmology* (1937), p. 168.

[23] Coffin, op. cit., p. 136.

[24] On Ficino's magico-musical theories, see D. P. Walker, op. cit. Of some small interest is Charles Butler's *Principles of Music* (1636), though this is of course a comparatively late work. Although he is mainly concerned with practical matters, Butler refers to the 'secret mysteries which lie hid in the profound Mathematik'. John Stevens in his article, 'Rounds and Canons from an Early Tudor Songbook' (*Music and Letters*, XXXII (1951), pp. 29–37), suggests that there was a Pythagorean group centred round William Cornysshe at the court of Henry VII. Concerning *musica speculativa* in France and elsewhere in this period see esp. Frances Yates, *French Academies*, op. cit., pp. 263–74.

[25] Cf. *Symposium* 186B–187C, p. 127 of Loeb edn., and Boethius *De Institutione Musica*, Bk I, sec. ii, ed. G. Friedlein, Leipzig, 1867, p. 188.

[26] Bruce Pattison, *Music and Poetry of the English Renaissance* (London, 1948), p. 71.

Notes

[27] As reported by Wittkower, op. cit., pp. 132–3.

[28] From the edn. of Edward Arber (Birmingham, 1865), p. 25–6.

[29] *Religio Medici*, II, sec. 9.

[30] *Sermon* 99, ed. L. P. Smith (1919), p. 162.

[31] *Utriusque Cosmi . . . historia* (1621), Tractat. I, lib. III, cap. III, p. 90.

[32] On which see esp. S. K. Heninger's important article, 'Some Renaissance versions of the Pythagorean Tetrad', *Stud. Ren. VIII* (1961), pp. 7–33.

[33] Fowler, op. cit., ch. IV, p. 24 ff.

[34] There were varying estimates of the length of the Platonic Great Year. The most widely accepted figure was in fact 36,000 years. See James Adam, *The Republic of Plato*, vol. II (Cambridge, 1929), pp. 201–9, for a full discussion.

[35] Marriage as an institution is a theme of the fifth book of the *Faerie Queene*. For its numerological features, see Fowler, op. cit., ch. V.

[36] Chapman, *Hero and Leander*, V, quoted from *Elizabethan Minor Epics*, ed. E. S. Donno (London, 1963), p. 114. Another extended example is in Drayton's *Endimion and Phoebe : Ideas Latmus*, lines 823–992 (Donno, p. 201 ff). Chapman's *The Amorous Zodiake* is numerologically structured; it is discussed by Fowler, op. cit., pp. 249–50.

[37] Bongo, *De Num. Myst.*, p. 260. 'But with one stone he struck the false Goliath the Philistine, while the latter was imprudently reviling the army of the living God; and knocked him flat. This is because in the one precept of charity the law is perfected.'

[38] For example, in Tyard's *Solitaire Second* discussed in Frances Yates, *French Academies*, p. 85 ff. The *Solitaire Second* is a theoretical treatise based on *Timaeus*, 35–6 and 41–2, concerning the proportioning of the world soul and the human soul, on the theme of the interlocking harmonies between the external physical world and the internal world of thought and feeling.

[39] I quote from J. A. Mazzeo, 'Cromwell as Davidic King', op. cit., ch. IX, p. 195, which brilliantly analyses the poem from this point of view.

[40] Hollander, op. cit., p. 243.

[41] *Poems*, ed Walker (Oxford, 1905), p. 253. Cowley's notes on the passage are on pp. 274–6.

[42] *Opera* (Basle, 1561), p. 614 as quoted by Yates, *French Academies*, p. 40. The passage appears also on p. 614 in the 1576 edn. Cf. also cap. xxi of the *De Vita Coelestis Comparanda*, p. 561 of the 1576 edn. We could well expect that where music and poetry come together most explicitly, i.e. in the musical setting of words, we might be most likely to find an explicit theory of numerological writing. But as Dr Fowler remarks, 'the existence of a well established numerological tradition in vocal music may have been a decisive factor in the growth of literary numerology: though our knowledge of the influence is not yet full enough to permit detailed conclusions' (op. cit., p. 240).

[43] For a fuller discussion of Henry More, see Røstvig, *Hidden Sense*, ch. V, p. 93 ff.

[44] Fowler, op. cit., p. 4.

[45] Another example of a numerological jeu d'esprit by Donne is his poem 'The Primrose'.

⁴⁶ A. Kent Hieatt, *Short Time's Endless Monument* (New York, 1960). Studies of numerological poetry before this date are Curtius' excursus in his *European Literature and the Latin Middle Ages* (tr. W. Trask, 1953), and Hopper's study of the *Divina Commedia* in his *Medieval Number Symbolism* (1938).

⁴⁷ Hieatt, op. cit., p. 46.

⁴⁸ Op. cit., pp. 49–50.

⁴⁹ Christopher Butler and Alastair Fowler, 'Time-beguiling Sport: Number Symbolism in Shakespeare's *Venus and Adonis*' in *Shakespeare 1564–1964*, Brown Univ. (1964), p. 124 ff.

⁵⁰ Even the total for the large numbers in the poem (28,000) refers to Southampton: for this is the number of minutes in 20 days (cf. lines 16, 240, 477–8, 517, 519, 522, 682, 775, and 833–4).

⁵¹ Miss Røstvig's interpretation of the *Nativity Ode* is in *The Hidden Sense*, p. 54 ff.

⁵² Alastair Fowler and Douglas Brooks, 'The Structure of Dryden's Ode for St Cecilia's Day 1687', *Essays in Criticism* (1967), p. 434 ff.

⁵³ Ludvig Spaeth, *Milton's Knowledge of Music* (1913, republished Ann Arbor, 1963), p. 58.

⁵⁴ W. C. Curry, *Milton's Ontology, Cosmology and Physics* (U. of Kentucky, Lexington, 1957).

⁵⁵ Bongo, op. cit., p. 434.

⁵⁶ Bongo, op. cit., pp. 416–21.

⁵⁷ I refer in what follows to his *Poetry and Numbers* (Lund, 1961), p. 88 ff.

⁵⁸ Op. cit., p. 93.

⁵⁹ I have found that these observations largely agree with those of Dr Fowler in his edition of *Paradise Lost* (London, 1968). In his notes on the numerology of the poem (pp. 440–3) he points out in addition, that books I–II and XI–XII are concerned with the consequences of a fall; and that the divine council of deliberation on man's fall and Christ's offer of mediation in III is answered by a council of judgment, and Christ's descent to judge and clothe fallen man in X. He also believes that the ten-book version of 1667 looks forward to the twelve-book version of 1674 in that in Book VII, line 21, of the earlier, we are told that 'Half yet remains unsung'—and this is true of the later version. The extreme length of Book X in 1667 also suggests that a twelve-book division was planned from the start.

Seven

Some Modern Developments, and the Aesthetic of Proportion

The preceding chapters will have presented to the reader a peculiarly one-sided picture of mathematical achievement from the Greeks to the Renaissance. The essentially philosophical, almost wilfully impractical quality of the tradition can perhaps be put into relief by mentioning a few of the more permanent, less mystical discoveries of the period. For instance, we have had no occasion to mention Pythagoras' theorem concerning the square upon the hypotenuse of a right-angled triangle, or many other deductions within Euclidean geometry, or Archimedes' hydrostatic principle. Indeed the mathematicians of Alexandria, of whom Archimedes was one, evolved a practically useful mathematics quite opposite to the static, contemplative, and theoretical achievements of the classical Greek age. We find Hipparchus, for example, using the principles of trigonometry to measure the size of the earth and the distance between the earth and moon.

Unfortunately, from about A.D. 500 to about A.D. 1400 there were no mathematicians in the Christian world to equal these, and any progress was made by Hindus and Arabs. But, as we have partly seen, at around the period of Copernicus' *De Revolutionibus* (1543), a mathematical revolution took place, and the most sophisticated mathematical techniques were in places allied to the numerological tradition. At about this time the practical problems of navigation, and of the velocities and ranges of cannon balls, and so on, were vigorously attacked by mathematicians, even by those otherwise as mystically inclined as John Dee, who lectured to mariners on problems of navigation at the newly founded Gresham's College. (We find a similar combination of practical and mystical in the Rosicrucian, Sir Isaac Newton.)

Similarly, Alberti's claim in *Della Pittura* (1435) that the first requirement of a painter was that he should know geometry, was not made simply in the service of the theories of proportion discussed above; the painter needed to know geometry in order to master the new system of perspective which was being taught by Brunelleschi to his pupils Masaccio, Donatello and Fra Filippo Lippi at the same period. From these artistic achievements was born the science of projective geometry, vital to mapmakers, who had to solve the problem of projecting figures from a sphere on to a flat sheet of paper. Thus Mercator's projection was evolved, which although it distorts the sizes of land masses at North and South, is useful for navigation since it preserves angles in a way that allows one to steer with constant compass bearings.

Even more impressive were the achievements of Galileo in defining the gravitational constant of attraction, as a functional, completely non-causal relationship, thus giving birth to an entirely new kind of mechanics, whose laws of motion revolutionized assumptions which had been in force since the time of Aristotle; and of Descartes, who as well as introducing a new type of radical scepticism into philosophy, created co-ordinate geometry.

These achievements, although they are clearly of an order distinct from the speculative numerology so far described, nevertheless gave birth in the work of Descartes and Leibniz to a new mathematical metaphysics largely shorn of theological assumptions and symbolic accretions. The new mathematics not only possessed that supreme clarity, certainty and indeed necessity so much sought after by metaphysicians, but it also found itself in that reciprocal relationship with rising scientific achievement which it still possesses.

Nevertheless, Pythagorean assumptions in science survived, at least as a possible method of attack on a problem. For the belief of Copernicus and Kepler, that we have a beautiful, ordered world with which to deal, corresponds in some measure to the ideal of simplicity and elegance in the theory by which we describe it. The test of the assumption lies in seeing which problems *will* yield to it. Of course we may believe that mathematics as a whole is the instrument to use, and we may believe that mathematics as a logical system automatically has 'Pythagorean' properties. But the true Pythagorean tries to simplify even further, to put quite severe constraints upon his mathematics (as we shall shortly see

Le Corbusier doing in architecture). He often has, for example, the problem of choosing between a particular numerical series, and a geometrical symmetry.[1] But it is difficult to see whether in considering the two possibilities, he is making a pragmatic assumption (embracing an hypothesis to which he is firmly attached), or is tied to a metaphysical principle (that the universe he is investigating is beautiful and ordered). Kepler made the second assumption when he believed that the creation of the universe took place according to a harmonic series. (In terms of the choice above, Kepler rejected symmetry, in his willingness to assign the paths of planets to ellipses, rather than the Platonically sanctioned spheres, and confined himself to the generation of a harmonic numerical series.) He was so little hampered by Plato's views on the possible ratios in this, that one may well agree with Rom Harré that what Kepler really brought to his investigations *a priori* was 'the methodological principle that harmonies are what count as the end of discovery.'[2]

In the modern period, Kepler was followed by Eddington, who was equally concerned to build the system of physical science about a few constants. (A constant is independent of any particular scale of measurement—thus if the gravitational constant of acceleration is 32 in the British system and 981 in the metric system, this is simply the consequence of the choice of a unit of measurement.) Eddington chose four fundamental constants which he thought would provide a 'scaling system' for both the small and large scale properties of the universe. These were: the ratio of the mass of the proton to the mass of the electron (value 1840), the ratio of particle action to radiation action (value 137), the ratio of gravitational attraction to electrical attraction (value 2.3×10^{39}), and the ratio of the radius of the curvature of space-time to the mean value of the wave (Schrödinger) for electron and proton (value 1.2×10^{39}). One can see to an extent why Eddington thought these constants fundamental, and how they are, as Kepler's harmonic series was not, dictated by very basic facts about the constitution of the universe. But as Harré points out, he was forced to do some fudging in his deductions of the ratios, which in any case are ultimately *contingent*, even if very pervasive, and are thus 'no more and no less contingent than any other *a posteriori* truths, they just require more negative evidence before they can be unseated'.[3]

Such considerations of scientific exactitude never bothered W. B. Yeats. His *A Vision* (first version, 1925, second, 1937) is in some ways remarkably similar to Giorgio's *Harmonie du Monde* or Kircher's *Musurgia Universalis* or any Renaissance astrological treatise. The latter, for all their fantasy elements, are fairly accurately founded on readings of classical texts, and try to preserve some consistency of meaning between them. Although Yeats is obviously trying to use some of these traditional elements in a number-symbolic way, the result is very confused and unclear. This despite, or perhaps because of the fact that Yeats and his wife, whose automatic writing formed the basis of the original version, had read Thomas Taylor's *Proclus*, 'a Latin work of Pico della Mirandola', Cornelius Agrippa, 'a great deal of medieval mysticism', and, for the later version, McKenna's translation of Plotinus. The doctrines of these earlier writers lose all hardness of outline in the roseate glow provided by Madam Blavatsky's theosophical writings, Boehme, Blake, and Swedenborg.

Indeed Yeats admits the primarily psychological basis of 'what must seem an arbitrary, harsh, and difficult symbolism. Yet such has always accompanied expression that unites the sleeping and waking mind'.[4] In this twilight area it is not surprising that the six wings of Daniel's angels, Pythagorean numbers, the Cabbala (in which the hairs in the beard of God are numbered) and John Dee's 'black scrying stone' seen by Dr Kelly, are confused. (We shall see shortly in examining some of the doctrines of the psychologist C. G. Jung, that expressions 'uniting the sleeping and waking mind' *can* be thought to have just this traditional character.)

Like Giorgio and Robert Fludd before him, Yeats is trying to subdue what is ultimately a vision of history to an aesthetic and astrological order, giving a Theosophist poet's answer to the Medieval and Renaissance reconciliation of Old and New Testaments within a divinely ordained historical order. He does not have the seven ages, or the musical harmonic framework of his predecessors; and so he regards his system, with its 28 phases, its cones and gyres, 'as stylistic arrangements of experience comparable to the cubes in the drawings of Wyndham Lewis and to the ovoids in the sculpture of Brancusi'.[5] Nevertheless he is sufficiently impressed by the *Timaeus* to claim that there are gyres of 'the same' and 'the other',[6] and to make his whole scheme fall within the Platonic Great Year to which he ascribes the value, in explicit opposition to Spenser, of 26,000 years.[7]

The basic conception in *A Vision* is that there are 28 phases of the moon, and that to these phases can be assigned different sets of psychological characteristics, which are combinations of the four faculties of Will, Mask, Creative Mind, and Body of Fate. (These are diagrammatically opposed in very much the same way as the Pythagorean tetrads discussed by Heninger.) Further, within each of these phases or incarnations, historical characters typically embody the differing combinations of the four faculties. This leads to some fairly odd collocations, such as Spinoza and Savanorola in phase 11, and Queen Victoria, Galsworthy and Lady Gregory in phase 24. As Yeats discusses these astrological phases he makes some often very sharp remarks about these characters, saying for example of Carlyle, who is bracketed with Dumas, James Macpherson and George Borrow, that he

> shows the phase at its worst. He neither could nor should have cared for anything but the personalities of history, but he used them as so many metaphors in a vast popular rhetoric, for the expression of thoughts that seeming his own were the work of preachers and angry ignorant congregations . . . Sexual impotence had doubtless weakened the *Body of Fate* and so strengthened the false *Mask*, yet one doubts if any mere plaster of ants' eggs could have helped where there was so great insincerity.[8]

There is some truth in his claim that he was the first to substitute for Biblical or mythological figures, historical movements and actual men and women, though Bongo's identification of Martin Luther with the Antichrist is perhaps a precedent. But the work is in fact most important (and sheds most light on his poems) as an idiosyncratic view of history, a temporal scheme interlocked by mathematical categories of astrological time. There is one further parallel between *A Vision* and the Renaissance, the age when some thought that the whole universe was hastening towards its end, 'all coherence gone'; for Yeats thought that each age was an expanding cone, which by centrifugal force was prone to disintegration:

> Turning and turning in the widening gyre
> The falcon cannot hear the falconer;
> Things fall apart; the centre cannot hold;
> Mere anarchy is loosed upon the world. . . .

James Joyce had read Yeats's *Vision*, as well as Madame Blavatsky and Vico, and they all influenced him in the cyclic structure and themes of *Finnegans Wake*. Hence the recurrence of the Blavatskyan number 432 or 4320 (the cycle of Book III closes at 4.32 a.m.). As Clive Hart remarks, 'Joyce was able to surpass even the ancient mystics in complexity and tortuousness. Like the mathematical world model of Minkowski, the great cycle of *Finnegans Wake* cannot be properly understood unless the distance between "events" is conceived in terms of both space and time'.[9] The book is thus numerologically structured; but the sources of that structure and their exact relevance are as yet obscure. Joyce has compounded our difficulties by superimposing three temporal schemes (as well he may in this Yeats-like dream vision): the account of a single day, of a typical week, and of a full liturgical year. (Spenser's and Shakespeare's sonnet sequences also have chronological schemes deriving from this latter source.) Joyce also uses imagery derived from the *Timaeus*. Shem and Shaun, the 'twinnt platonic yearlings' are called 'the same' and 'the other' respectively.[10] The extent of Joyce's learning, and his intention to combine all the arts in his work, are seen in his parody at this point of a Renaissance treatise, garnished in the margin with a madly profuse citation of authorities:

> Steady steady steady steady steady studiavamus. Many many many many many manducabimus. We've had our day at triv and quad and writ our bit as intermidgets.

As indeed Joyce had.

Joyce also uses a temporal symbolic organization of his work in the plot of the *Portrait of the Artist*, and in the Oxen of the Sun episode in *Ulysses*. The model is in each case the nine months of gestation, which in *Ulysses* is suggested by an elaborate series of parodies of English prose styles in historical order, from Anglo-Saxon to Pater and Ruskin.[11] The chapter begins with a set of three incantations three times repeated, symbolizing the nine months. As Mr Bloom remarks 'do anything you like with figures juggling'—the number, seven, of his house in Eccles Street is a 'mystic number', and Stephen plays on the brothel piano a cycle of 'hollow fifths' which is 'the ultimate return', since a cycle of fifths will go in order through the possible scales. I doubt whether, as Gilbert suggests, the octave is meant here as a reconciliation between the Pythagorean limit and unlimit, though Gilbert has a special authority in these matters.[12] The tenth episode of *Ulysses*, 'The Wandering Rocks', is, as again Gilbert tells us, a 'small scale model' of the rest of the book, for both it and the book have eighteen episodes, typographically distinguished by stars, and the episodes of 'Wandering Rocks' contain sentences taken from other parts of the book. Joyce may well have chosen the tenth episode for this technique, as it is a tetraktyc number containing all others. It is perhaps significant that the seventh of these eighteen mini-episodes contains all the numbers up to seven. As John Eglinton remarks, 'Seven is dear to the mystic mind.'[13]

One cannot claim that Joyce's number symbolism is particularly clear, because it is so well buried in the complexity of his other concerns. But it seems that in *Finnegans Wake* at least, there are some basic patterns to be discerned. We need not expect them to be imbued with traditional numerological symbolism, they are, rather, psychologically significant organizing devices. The explanation of Joyce's attraction to cycles, crosses, quincunxes, and so on, is more likely to be accounted for by the Jungian depth psychology of which he was well aware, though unwilling to admit it.[14]

Jung indeed has a great deal to say about basic number symbols and diagrams, and does so with reference to many of the sources discussed in this book. Thus for example he says that the cross symbolizes the four directions by which a man can find his bearings, hence in the domain of psychological processes it functions as an organizing centre. Nevertheless the cross presents a man-made and artificial division which is opposed to the unconscious and purely natural unity of the circle. The cross is the *complexio oppositorum* on which man must be stretched and the 'old man' must die if he is to be whole and to live. (He refers us to the Epistles to the Romans 6:6, Ephesians 4:22, Colossians 3:9.) Thus according to the theory of analytical psychology, objects in dreams, such as four-legged tables, public squares, cruciform buildings, and so on, can be taken to connote the basic psychic properties of quaternities, trinities, squares, the *homo quadratus* without blemish, and other symbols, which in various ways are projections of the self.

Indeed Jung finds that most of the basic number symbols discussed in this book occur in dreams, as 'archetypes', and interprets them very much according to Renaissance sources, though predominantly alchemical ones, to which he adds the contribution of Eastern religion, especially concerning the geometrically designed mandala symbols. By an 'archetype' he means motives that repeat themselves in the mythology and folk-lore of different peoples. They are collective phenomena which are both constituents of myths and autochthonous individual products of unconscious origin, transmitted to us by heredity. It is as the latter that they can occur spontaneously in our dreams. But it is often difficult to see how Jung's interest in the history of numerological ideas connects with his belief that they have a part to play in psychotherapy.

He seems to maintain: (a) that patients spontaneously have dreams containing quaternities, etc.; (b) that these symbols or archetypes are explicable essentially by the tradition described in this book; (c) that the patient who dreams does not know the analyst's explanation beforehand, yet that in some way (since these symbols are 'archetypes') they have the psychological function in dreams that they had in the original tradition. The claim is that patients dream with these symbols who could not possibly have any acquaintance with Pythagoras, or alchemy. The logically disputable step is (c), both because of its assumption concerning spontaneously occurring archetypes (it may be doubted whether they are biologically inherited) and because one wonders whether patients are not being *taught* in some way to have dreams of the right type. (The old objection that those treated by Freudians have Freudian dreams, and those treated by Jungians have Jungian ones.) It may be doubted whether even the most neurotic of us have dreams or fantasies in terms of Renaissance alchemy. On the other hand, the evidence Jung cites from his case-histories is extremely impressive.

I shall take as an example his discussion of quaternity in his Terry lectures on 'Psychology and Religion' (1938) which has the advantage of being a clear exposition meant to be intelligible even to those who do not have some acquaintance with his work as a whole.[15]

The content of the symbol will be familiar to us: it is its psychological function which Jung describes in a new way. Though his view of symbols as agents for the integration of the personality would come as no surprise to a Renaissance magus or alchemist; compare what we said in Chapter III about the magus and the *vis imaginativa*. Jung in fact sees it as part of his mission to recall men to some of these old truths.

Thus one of his patients dreamt of groups of four pyramids, 'always alluding to an idea akin to the Pythagorean tetraktys'. He goes on in this second lecture to refer to the sources of the Pythagorean doctrine, to four in Christian iconology and in Gnosticism, and to the four elements and humours in alchemy. He tells us that in the dream the quaternity is a 'significant exponent of the religious cult created by the unconscious mind', which is 'capable at times of assuming an intelligence and purposiveness which are superior to actual conscious insight'.[16] The claim that Jung makes, is that the religious unconscious is stocked with inherited symbols of this type, and that in dreams it has a 'voice' not identical with the conscious ego.

Thus one may dream of the Pythagorean tetraktys as a symbol of 'self-collection' under the guise of a circle divided into four main parts, or a flower, a square place or room, four people in a boat, four chairs around a table, a wheel with eight spokes, a 'world clock' or in many other ways that Jung cites.[17] He asserts that he has encountered many separate cases of this, in which 'Number symbolism and its venerable history is a field of knowledge utterly beyond the interests of our dreamer's mind'.[18] But this knowledge allows the analyst, aware of the numerological tradition, to diagnose images of the circle or globe containing four divisions as signifying the Deity (i.e. the God of Nicholas of Cusa, 'cuius centrum est ubique, circumferentia vero nusquam', who created perfect spheres in the *Timaeus*, and interlocked within them the four elements). Yet the patient, unaware of these facts, takes the image to symbolize himself or something in himself. On this evidence, Jung tells us that it is mere prejudice to believe that the Deity is outside man—the image really signifies the God within.[19] Jung goes on: 'I cannot omit calling attention to the interesting fact that whereas the central Christian symbol is a Trinity, the formula of the unconscious mind is a quaternity.'[20] (A curious extension of speculation concerning God's nature; compare our remarks concerning the evolution of the doctrine of the Trinity in Chapter II!)[21] The added fourth constituent, he says, is the feminine aspect, earth and woman, the anima, and it provides the final clue to the solution of the patient's problem: avoidance of the suppressed anima, partly but unsuccessfully overlaid by a religious concern. He thus implicitly criticizes the doctrine of the Trinity, as lacking any representation of the 'inferior function' of the anima, which it can only do if expanded into a quaternity.[22]

An extremely conscious use of structural numbers, whose psychological or symbolic basis is hardly open to inspection, occurs in Berg's *Concerto for Piano, Violin, and thirteen Wind Instruments* of 1925. This work everywhere alludes to the 'Trinity' of the second Viennese school (i.e. Schoenberg and his disciples Berg and Webern), for as we shall see, it uses three and its multiples with incredible ingenuity. But this seems not to be with any mystical or symbolic intent; Berg's aim seems to have been to impose a quite abstract aesthetic of proportion upon the whole work. (Compare, for example the symmetrical construction of Bartok's fourth and fifth quartets, in the latter of which the sections of movement V reflect those of I and those of IV reflect II. There are symmetrical features within movements too; the third part of I in the fifth quartet presents the themes of the first part in reverse order, and inverted.)

There are even numerical coincidences surrounding the production of Berg's concerto—he had intended to present Schoenberg with the full score on his fiftieth birthday (13 September 1924) and in fact completed the short score on his own fortieth birthday (9 February 1925). Such symbolism as there is is rather private. Thus Berg in his 'open letter' to Schoenberg of 9 February 1925 remarks that the number of instruments involved, fifteen, is 'a holy kind of number for this kind of instrumental composition since your opus 9'. (Schoenberg's *Chamber Symphony* No. 1.)[23] The three main tone-row themes of the work are a kind of gematria. They incorporate as far as possible the letters of the names of (I) ArnolD S(Es, i.e. E♭)CHonBErG, (II) Anton wEBErn, and (III) AlBAn BErG. In fact the notes of (Webern) and (Berg) are all contained in the (Schoenberg) tone-row, thus, as Redlich points out, symbolizing the bonds of friendship between the three composers and their acceptance of Schoenberg as master.[24] We find similar allusions to names in Schumann's *Carnaval* and *Abegg* variations, and in Liszt's Prelude and Fugue on the name of B-A-C-H, and other works.

Berg points out in his letter that the number of bars in the whole work and in its individual sections 'was also determined by divisibility by three—I realize that—in so far as I make this generally known—my reputation as a mathematician will grow in proportion (. . . to the square of the distance) as my reputation as a composer sinks'.[25] Thus the work has 3 movements and uses instruments in the 3 categories of keyboard, strings, and wind. The first movement has 30 bars of thematic exposition, the second is in ternary form, and the third has three basic rhythms. Indeed the number three is the structural basis for nearly every detail of the concerto. The structural analysis (adapted from Berg's open letter) is as follows. (The numbers are numbers of bars.)

    I Thema con variazioni. Theme (30) var 1 (30) var 2 (60) var 3 (30) var 4 (30) var 5 (60)—the total number of bars being 240.

    II Adagio. Tripartite. A1 (30) B (12 + 36 + 12) A2, (an inversion of A1) (30) A2 (30) B (this time as a mirror reflection: 12 + 36 + 12) A1 (30)—the total again 240, making 480 for the first two movements.

    III Rondo Ritmico. This is a compound of I and II. Introduction and Cadenza (54) Exposition (96) Development (79). The last two are repeated, followed by a recapitulation and coda of 76 bars, adding up to 480, the total for the first two movements, the whole work containing 960 bars all told.

My last example of a modern exponent of numerological structures is the architect Le Corbusier. Thus we see that the same arts as were affected by numerology in the Renaissance, music, architecture and literature, have their modern counterparts. Le Corbusier naturally progressed from his early association with cubism and the paintings containing machine-like forms of his friend Leger, to a fascination with the golden section. This is a ratio of proportion between numbers, which can be expressed in geometrical areas, which has long been supposed to be in some way more aesthetically pleasing than any other. The golden section is generated from a single number, $\dfrac{1 + \sqrt{5}}{2} = 1\cdot618$, usually called ø in the modern literature concerning it. Its chief property is, that multiplied by itself it gives $2\cdot617924$, in fact itself plus 1, so that this third number is the sum of the preceding two (1 and ø). By proceeding similarly (i.e. ø × ø, ø × ø × ø etc.), we can in fact generate a series in which each number except unity, from which it starts, is the sum of the preceding two. A simpler version of this is the Fibonacci series using whole numbers, 1, 2, 3, 5, 8, 13, 21 and so on, which has exactly the same additive properties as the ø progression. Now Le Corbusier thought that buildings could be both beautiful and supremely well adapted to use by man if they were built on a scale embodying the golden section series, based upon the height of a man. He originally took as a man's height $1\cdot75$m, but a certain M. Py remarked to him:

> Isn't the ($1\cdot75$m) value a French height? Have you never noticed that in English detective novels, the good looking men, such as the policemen, are always 6 feet tall?
> We tried to apply this standard: Six feet = 6 × 30.48 = 182·88cm. To our delight, the graduations of a new 'Modulor' based on a man 6 feet tall, translated themselves before our eyes into round figures in feet and inches.[26]

The number $182\cdot88$ was significant for Le Corbusier because it fell within a usable golden section series representing the proportions of a man with arm upraised—from the top of his head to the tips of his upraised fingers 43 cm, from his head to his navel 70 cm, from navel to ground 113 cm, from head to ground 183 cm, from navel to ground 113 cm, from head to ground, 183 cm. Another useful golden series generated by the man 183 cm tall, was from ground to genitals 86 cm, from genitals to tip of upraised fingers 140 cm, the total from ground to fingers being 226 cm. These two sets of components correspond to the two series named by Le Corbusier the 'Red' and the 'Blue' series.[27] The coincidence of the man 6 feet tall with a golden series expressed in centimetres, led Le Corbusier to claim that he had reconciled the British and metric scales of measurement.[28]

Thus like the Renaissance builders of churches described earlier, the modern architect could create like a God in the image of man: 'From the start we had declared: Behind the wall, the gods play; they play with numbers, of which the universe is made up.'[29]

Nevertheless the Modulor series was not intended to convey an occult symbolism; Le Corbusier, had he known of the Biblical doctrines concerning the proportions of the Ark, would have been interested but unimpressed. He wished, in a machine age of mass-produced building materials, to have some principle for the selection and order of the sizes of those materials, such that when used in combination, they would be both beautiful, and, since the golden series contains the proportions of a man, well adapted to the design of buildings (and even furniture), which are 'either containers of man or extensions of man'.[30]

Le Corbusier has in fact been responsible for the erection of buildings whose proportions have been dictated throughout by the scale of the golden section based on the height of a man, the Modulor. They are his chapel at Ronchamp of 1950–3, apartment blocks at Berlin (where the system was not in fact completely carried through) and Nantes, the Brazilian pavilion at the Univercity City in Paris, 1957–8, and the Secretariat, Palace of Justice and other buildings at Chandigarh, administrative capital of the Punjab, at the foot of the Himalayas (1953 onwards). All these buildings have the tremendous distinction of a great architect, whose designs even before the period in which he became interested in the Modulor, have always been revolutionary, and resulted in buildings of great beauty.

But in saying this, one wonders exactly why we think that a building by Le Corbusier, or Berg's concerto, or the form of *Finnegans Wake,* have any aesthetic value, and to ask this is to ask what the theoretical basis of any 'aesthetic of proportion' may be. So I should like to conclude by developing the argument of Chapter V concerning aesthetic assumptions—which was presented in strictly Renaissance terms—into a critique of the numerological aesthetic.

The evidence presented in this book has shown, I hope, that there has been both in the Renaissance and modern periods a tradition of artistic creation according to numbers. In the earlier period this tradition had considerable cohesion: it had its basic texts, fairly faithfully transmitted, and it was thus enriched by the motives of philosophic, scientific and theological speculation. It gave to the arts a wealth of meanings drawn from 'a genealogy of wisdom'. In the modern period we have seen that these symbolic meanings are often changed, but that there is nevertheless belief in an aesthetic of proportion, in the numerical structuring of works of art. Creation according to these methods has clearly stimulated a number of major artists. (From here on I hope that what I say will apply as well to the Renaissance as to the modern period.) These artists made an *a priori* assumption that the world with which they had to deal was capable of being given a numerical order, and that the work of art could reflect this. In the case of literature this is clearly deliberate, for words, unlike building materials, obviously do not have to have mathematical properties. But one may feel that an architect using the Modulor, or designing a church as Giorgio did, simply has to have *some* principle of order and proportion upon which to proceed, and it does not much matter which one he chooses, in terms of aesthetic *effect*. The mere use of the golden section, for example, may guarantee nothing.

But surely there is more to it than this: and so the basic problem in justifying an 'aesthetic of proportion' (which I simply use as a convenient label for all the artistic techniques so far described), lies in showing that it does produce a distinctively valuable kind of response in its audience. The hope of many practitioners was of course that such proportions as those of the golden section would guarantee beauty, indeed provide an objective standard for it. But I think it can be shown that all *non-symbolic* systems of proportion are in fact arbitrary (the non-arbitrariness of symbolic systems consists in their having a relatively fixed verbal meaning). As Gombrich has shown, even the 'science of perspective' is really only a particular way of working an illusion upon us,[31] and it offers no more certain an insight into nature than Eddington's attempted deduction of Pythagorean constants. Systems of architectural proportion based on the human scale suffer from the same defects: they do little more than satisfy a demand for scientific exactitude, allied to 'humanism' in a weak sense. As Arnheim remarks:

> Unfortunately . . . the human figure cannot be standardized, and since the stature of any population is distributed in a bell-like curve, it seems ludicrous to

specify the relation between man and his objects to the
fraction of an inch.[32]

It seems that only one's tailor can correctly observe one of the
basic principles of the Modulor. Though in defence of Le Corbusier it must be said that his choice of a six-foot-tall policeman
as model allows for the greatest possible convenient use of his
buildings. Or to take the problem the other way round: however
beautiful an artist's proportions for a human being may seem to
us, it is clear that there are very few *actual* human beings who
conform to the scale, and that many others are nevertheless
beautiful.

Indeed this type of system of proportion based on arbitrary
premises (both concerning the human scale, and on the unproven
premise that the golden section or musical harmonic intervals
expressed in spatial terms are in fact uniquely aesthetically satisfying) may also turn out to have unnecessarily restrictive consequences. Objects produced in accordance with them may lack
some of the qualities open to artists who explore a wider range of
possibilities. (Compare Le Corbusier's sets of panels based on
Modulor proportions with the geometrical abstractions of Mon-
drian or Victor Pasmore.) Le Corbusier of course tries to gain
flexibility by using two golden series, but the fact remains that the
combination of units is not very well taken care of, since very few
of the Modulor dimensions are multiples of one another.

So far what we have said is negative, and is open to a very
simple objection by the artist, be he architect or writer or musician
—'Why shouldn't I proceed on restrictive assumptions? It makes
my work easier, and like the scientist I may be able to discover far
more by using a simple and elegant "hypothesis".' This seems a
fair reply, but one must remember that it has more to do with the
psychology of creation than with making any assertion about the
superior value of the aesthetic product. But even so, with regard
to the latter, there is a great deal that is positive to be said.

It does seem that we prefer *unified* aesthetic objects, and that
systems of proportion may be a way (but not the only way) of
guaranteeing that unity, such that, as Vitruvius and others have
said, nothing can be taken away without damaging the harmony
of the whole. One may well expect that in so far as systems of
proportion do not dictate the shapes themselves and their sizes,

but the *relationships* between them, these latter may well turn out to be 'binding' ones. There may be, so to speak, a guarantee of 'Gestalt', a satisfactory opening and closing of the aesthetic experience.[33] The resulting proportions may give us; balance and unity, making for 'tranquillity'; clarity and simplicity, making for 'orientation'; and variety and tension, making for 'stimulation'.[34] Now even if these types of correlations between perceptual qualities and responses are accepted as intuitively plausible, they are very difficult to verify. Thus, for example we may say that a golden section rectangle divided in the dimensions 8:5 has 'unity' or 'tension', while a 2:1 rectangle threatens to break up. But how *objective* is our perception of visual planes (or perhaps phrase structures in music, or even stanzas in a poem), as balanced, reposeful, and so on? Is the statement 'The golden section makes a good proportion' even as well entrenched in our language as an acceptable statement, as 'blue recedes and red advances'? Such tests as have been made of unprompted golden-section judgments are not very encouraging. Very early on (1876) Fechner found that subjects preferred golden-section rectangles when asked (they won 35% of choices between 10 rectangles), and yet that as far as pictures in museums were concerned, a considerably shorter rectangle was preferred (5:4 upright or 4:3 horizontal). Many more modern experiments have proved to be equally inconclusive: trained artists prefer more complex and less symmetrical figures, which tends to show that the more sophisticated you are, the less you prefer at least the simpler types of balance or symmetry. (The main fault of psychological experiments from our point of view is that they necessarily use very simple shapes and combinations of them to test preferences.) One must remember that in actual pictures and buildings *geometrical* symmetry producing balance and so on, is not the only relevant element. The 'weight' of the colours or the importance of various parts of the subject of the picture or functions of the building may also make for a kind of balance. There is also the function of suggested movement to be taken into account. Nevertheless the properties of 'balance', 'equilibrium' and so on, do seem to be 'pro-words' in the evaluation of at least some works of art, though perhaps they are usually applied to more complex objects than a simple theory of geometrical or linear proportion might allow.[35]

A fundamental problem lies in dealing with these rather

abstract emotional correlates of formal properties. It seems that this relationship may be clearer in music than in architecture or painting. For music, although we tend to think of it as a continuous stream of sound which sets up expectations and fulfils them by harmony and rhythm, has nevertheless always had clear structural nodal points.[36] We can recognize the return of a tune, or a new variation upon it, the beginning of a development, a recapitulation, a coda, and so on. These can all be important *dramatic* events. The problem is, can we also learn to recognize proportional nodal points as such? (In the case of Berg's *Chamber Concerto*, for example.) In music at least up to the rise of the 'second Viennese school' there has always been a kind of proportion and symmetry on the small scale, hence the prevalence for example of four-bar phrases (and the peculiar difficulties Brahms set himself in using a five-bar theme for his *St Antoni Variations*).[37] What seems to be needed is some qualitative change at the proportional nodal points. The excessive care for symmetry in Berg's *Chamber Concerto* can be seen to be very largely a conscious use of structural techniques that had been quite traditionally used in earlier works, but not in the service of some theory. For example, the main sections of Bach's Chaconne in D minor for violin approximate to the golden section; or the first part of the scherzo of Bruckner's Eighth Symphony is an elaborate symmetrical structure built up of 2- 4- 6- and 8-bar phrases into a balanced 32 + 32 bar sequence.[38] Even music that seems not to be susceptible of this sort of division, to be an unending stream of melody, such as the Prelude to *Tristan and Isolde*, has a symmetrical structure. Here the phrase of bars 17–21 returns three times in identical form in different places, each time more forcefully, and these repetions occur at exactly equal distances. The reader is referred to Leichtentritt's analysis for examples of further proportions in this apparently free-flowing piece.[39] The important point is that these proportional features of the *Tristan and Isolde* prelude are correlated to 'expressive' qualities; they represent peaks and relaxations of emotional tension, important thematic transformations, and so on, and this is by and large the case for the important proportional nodal points in the Berg piece. If these nodal points are *not* perceived in some such way, one can only say that they must be a stimulus to composition, or have some disputable subconscious (intuited) effect upon the listener.

Having involved ourselves in a terminology of 'nodal points' and 'expressive qualities', it is perhaps apposite to attempt a form/content distinction, of which that is a variation, which will also allow us to consider numerically structured literature. We have seen that in the 'aesthetic of proportion': (1) 'form' may be correlated with more (architecture, painting) or less (music) impalpable emotional responses, such as 'repose' or 'tension' or 'equilibrium' of opposing forces. (2) There is a 'content' where there is a reference from the formal properties of the work to some intellectual (verbal) system. This type of content may be called 'secondary' as opposed to the 'primary' content, e.g. the primary content of *Epithalamion* is Spenser's marriage as opposed to the hidden astronomical argument of the poem. This type of secondary 'content' for numerologically structured works leads to perfectly acceptable and relatively uncontroversial *explanations of the meaning* of the work on some level or another—in fact the usual interpretative work of the critic. Though of course there have to be some ground rules—in the case of literature, the structural divisions of the work must be clearly discriminable and lead to a constant system of measurement (e.g. we don't make a stanza-count based on astronomical numbers in one part of the poem and one based on musical harmonic numbers in another, without good reason). We also want to make sure that the symbolic meaning of a structural number (especially if we break it down, e.g. by factorization) has the sanction of some contemporary authority. And most importantly, this interpretation on the allegoric level must be supported by the primary literal meaning of the text. These ground rules help us to avoid reading out of the work, what we have just put into it. (The same sorts of considerations concerning the probable creative method and symbolic intent of the artist should prevent us doing this in the case of architecture.)

There is of course a difficulty in showing how the numerical structure of a poem affects our continuous reading of it. It may not structure our experience in the way that symmetries in music do. In reading *Finnegans Wake* or Chapman's *Amorous Zodiak* we do get some sense of a measured passing of time, but the real force of the number symbolism lies in our understanding the work on more than one level. There is then perhaps a psychological problem of integrating the knowledge derived from the interpretation into our continuous reading of the text. But this seems to apply to nearly all types of critical interpretation, as opposed to critical explanation.

A recurrent characteristic of these number-symbolic interpretations is that they initiate us into a 'world picture', one in which, whether it involves a 'Platonic ascent' to a world of mathematical forms (as in the case of a Renaissance church) or an awareness of the world as controlled by magic and astrology (Agrippa) or the phases of the moon (Yeats), we do not, on the whole, believe. Critical interpretation has to teach us to respond to this sympathetically.

This leads me to a final distinction which I think is crucial to the understanding of the 'aesthetic of proportion'. It concerns the character of our response, which is either (a) taught (as in the case of the allegorizing world-view mentioned above) or (b) intuitive (as when Alberti and others claim that through the eye one can be put in touch with musical harmony and indeed the fundamental laws of the universe).

The intuitive approach essentially involves all the problems of the 'Gestalt' of symmetrical and golden-section objects, discussed above. A further consideration which may lead one to believe that these supposedly intuitive responses are in fact taught, is supplied by Scholfield—he says that if the use of systems of proportion

> was the result of intuition, one would expect the same types of relationships to have appeared spontaneously in all periods of good design. In fact, this is not the case, and the sorts of mathematical relationships which occur are closely related to the mathematical knowledge of the period.[40]

The same sorts of considerations apply in the case of our response to psychological archetypes. Can we not *help* responding at some profound level to the numerological and cyclical organization of Joyce's literary dream, just as Jung's patients did to theirs? I think that one has to say that as far as these intuitive or subconscious responses are concerned, the theories of analytical psychology are at best a plausible hypothesis. They are of course the source of a perfectly respectable conscious technique of *interpretation*, especially in the cases where the artist can be shown to be acquainted with the theory, as Joyce was. (The same sorts of considerations apply to pictures embodying quaternity symbols, mandalas, and so on, but not I think to music.)

In conclusion, one must say, whatever reservations one may have concerning the aesthetic of numerological proportion, that it seems clear that the very great works of art created in accordance with this aesthetic are capable of providing an enormous enrichment of our experience, once the ideas that surround them are understood.

Notes

[1] Cf. H. Weyl, *Symmetry* (Princeton and Oxford, 1952).

[2] Rom Harré, *The Anticipation of Nature* (London, 1965), p. 86. I am indebted to him in the following discussion of Eddington.

[3] Harré, op. cit., p. 91. On the deduction of the constant 137, cf. pp. 88–90.

[4] W. B. Yeats, *A Vision* (edn. of 1962), p. 23.

[5] Op. cit., p. 25.

[6] Op. cit., pp. 68–9.

[7] Op. cit., p. 202, cf. pp. 212–13, 248–9. There are extended sections on the Great Year in ed. of 1925, p. 149 ff, and in ed. of 1937, p. 243 ff. They differ considerably.

[8] Op. cit., p. 116.

[9] Clive Hart, *Structure and Motive in Finnegans Wake* (London, 1962), pp. 64–5. I am indebted to him in the discussion which follows, despite some small disagreements. Hart itemizes other associations for numbers on his p. 186 ff. They are not number-symbolic in a traditional way but refer to characters or constellations of characters in the book, e.g. 5 is the Four Men and their Ass, though 111 signifies Anna Livia Plurabelle's children and her own name by gematria. The diagram which Hart interprets as derived from Plato's world soul (*FW*, p. 293), is more plausibly to be interpreted as a parody of diagrams in *A Vision*, the first edition of which had attacked Joyce as an example of the disintegration of the unified consciousness which had characterized earlier artists (pp. 211–12 (1925)—omitted from later editions).

[10] *Finnegans Wake* (edn. of 1950), pp. 293, 300. This theme is developed by Hart, op. cit., p. 133 f. When Shaun is superimposed on the five provinces (475 f.) he is Sir Thomas Browne's quincunx, and Vitruvian man, the human microcosm such as Joyce would have found it in Agrippa, Leonardo, and Vitruvius, whom he had read.

[11] For the technique in the *Portrait*, see R. Ellman, *James Joyce* (1959), pp. 306–9.

[12] Stuart Gilbert, *James Joyce's Ulysses* (Harmondsworth, 1963), p. 69 n.

[13] *Ulysses* (1937), p. 173.

[14] See Ellman, op. cit., pp. 480–3, 688–9, 691–3. Joyce refused to be analysed by Jung, but his daughter was for a time Jung's patient. His explicit references to Freud and Jung in *Finnegans Wake* are disparaging.

[15] The lectures are published by Yale U.P. (1938). References to numerological topics are scattered throughout Jung's *Collected Works*. An important paper is 'On the significance of Number dreams' in Vol. IV of that edition.

[16] *Psychology and Religion* (1938), pp. 44–6.

[17] Op. cit., p. 65.

[18] Op. cit., p. 65.

[19] Op. cit., p. 71–2.

[20] Op. cit., p. 73.

[21] Jung goes more deeply into the psychological basis of the traditional Christian doctrine of the Trinity as opposed to his concept of a more complex quaternity containing the 'feminine principle', in his 'A psychological approach to the doctrine of the Trinity', *Collected Works*, Vol. XI, pp. 109 ff.

[22] Cf. Jung, *Psychology and Religion*, pp. 76–7 and 90–1. Jung's views on this topic are discussed by Victor White, O.P., in his *Soul and Psyche* (1960), ch. 6. In the following two chapters he goes on to discuss the doctrine of the 'missing feminine'. He begins his discussion—'A wit has remarked that what Freud did for sex, Jung did for the Number Four'.

[23] Quoted from W. Reich, *Alban Berg* (London, 1965), p. 143.

[24] H. F. Redlich, *Alban Berg* (London, 1957), p. 120.

[25] Reich, op. cit., p. 147.

[26] Le Corbusier, *Modulor* 1 (London, 1954), p. 56.

[27] Le Corbusier, *Modulor* 2 (London, 1958), pp. 58–61.

[28] *Modulor* 1, p. 17.

[29] *Modulor* 2, p. 17.

[30] *Modulor* 1, p. 60.

[31] E. H. Gombrich, *Art and Illusion* (London, 1962), ch. 8.

[32] R. Arnheim, *Towards a Psychology of Art* (London, 1967), p. 108.

[33] For the application of Gestalt theory to painting, see R. Arnheim, *Art and Visual Perception* (London, 1956), and to music, see L. Meyer, *Emotion and Meaning in Music* (University of Chicago Press, 1956).

[34] Arnheim, op. cit., p. 103.

[35] Cf. C. W. Valentine, *The Experimental Psychology of Beauty* (London, 1962), ch. 5. Information theory may be coming up with some of the answers to these questions as applied to the arts, since it sees what they communicate as an optimum mixture of order and disorder, or redundancy and information. Cf. the symposium on 'Information Theory and the Arts', *Journal of Aesthetics and Art Criticism*, XVII (June 1955).

[36] For this expectation and fulfilment model see Meyer, op. cit.

[37] Cf. Hugo Leichtentritt, *Musical Form* (Harvard, 1959), chs. 1 and 2, concerning the regular and irregular construction of musical phrases.

[38] Cf. Leichtentritt, op. cit., p. 390 (the whole of his extended analysis of this work is relevant).

[39] Op. cit., p. 355 ff.

[40] P. H. Scholfield, *The Theory of Proportion in Architecture* (1958), p. 1.

Select Bibliography

I Primary Sources

AGRIPPA, HENRY CORNELIUS, *De occulta philosophia libri tres*, Antwerp and Paris, 1531. English translation, London, 1651.

ALBERTI, LEON BATTISTA, *Ten Books on Architecture*, tr. James Leoni, London, 1726. Facsimile edition, J. Rykovert, London, 1955.

ARISTOTLE, *Metaphysics*, ed. W. D. Ross, Oxford, 1924.

—— *De Caelo*, tr. W. K. C. Guthrie, London and Cambridge (Mass.), 1960.

AUGUSTINE, St, *The City of God*, tr. John Healey, ed. R. G. V. Tasker, London and New York, 1960.

—— *De musica*, tr. R. C. Tagliaferro, Annapolis, 1939.

BOETHIUS, *De arithmetica*, ed. and commentary Girardus Rufus, Paris, 1521.

—— *De musica*, ed. Oscar Paul, Leipzig, 1872.

BONGO, PIETRO, *Mysticae numerorum significationis liber*, Bergamo, 1585. Expanded ed., Basel, 1618, entitled *De Numerorum Mysteria*.

DONNE, JOHN, *Essays in Divinity*, ed. E. M. Simpson, Oxford, 1952.

DU BARTAS, SALUSTE, *Divine Weekes and Workes*, tr. Joshua Sylvester, London, 1613.

FICINO, MARSILIO, *Opera Omnia*, Basel, 1576.

FLUDD, ROBERT, *Utriusque cosmi historia scilicet et minoris metaphysica, physica atque technica historia*, Oppenheim, 1621.

GAFURIO, FRANCHINO, *Theoria musicae*, Venice, 1492.

GIORGIO, FRANCESCO, *De harmonia mundi totius cantica tria*, Paris, 1545, tr. Guy le Fevre de la Boderie, *L'Harmonie du Monde*, Paris, 1579. (Followed by a translation of Pico's *Heptaplus*.)

GOULART, SIMON, *A Learned Summary upon the Famous Poem of Saluste, Lord of Bartas*, tr. Thomas Lodge, London, 1621.

HUGH OF ST VICTOR, *Exegetica*, in Migne, *Patrologia latina*, 175.

IAMBLICHUS (i.e. PSEUDO-IAMBLICHUS), *Theologumena arithmetica*, ed. V. de Falco, Leipzig, 1922.

INGPEN, WILLIAM, *The Secrets of Numbers*, London, 1624.

KEPLER, JOHANNES, *Mysterium cosmographicum*, Tubingen, 1596.

—— *Harmonice mundi*, Linz, 1619.

—— *Epitome*, Paris, 1622.

KIRCHER, ATHANASIUS, *Musurgia universalis sive ars magna consoni et dissoni in x libros digesta*, Rome, 1650.

—— *Arithmologia: sive de abditis numerorum mysteriis*, Rome, 1665.

MACROBIUS, *Commentary on the Dream of Scipio*, tr. and ed. W. H. Stahl, New York, 1952.

MARTIANUS CAPELLA, *De Nuptiis Philologiae et Mercurii*, ed. A. Dick, Leipzig, 1925.

NICOMACHUS OF GERASE, *Introduction to Arithmetic*, tr. M. L. D'Ooge, University of Michigan Studies in the Human Sciences, Vol. 16, 1926.

PACIOLI, LUCA, *De divina proportione*, Venice, 1509.

PLATO, *Timaeus*, tr. H. D. P. Lee, Harmondsworth, 1965.

PLOTINUS, *Enneads*, tr. S. McKenna, rev. B. S. Page, 3rd ed., London, 1962.

VITRUVIUS, *On Architecture*, tr. and ed. Frank Granger, 2 vols., London, 1931.

WOTTON, SIR HENRY, *Elements of Architecture*, London, 1624.

2 Studies relevant to the history of number symbolism, and to numerological criticism

ALLERS, RUDOLF, 'Microcosmus' in *Traditio*, II (1944), pp. 319–407.

ARMSTRONG, A. H., ed., *The Cambridge History of Later Greek and Early Medieval Philosophy*, Cambridge, 1967.

ARNHEIM, RUDOLF, *Towards a Psychology of Art*, London, 1967.

BLAU, J. L., *The Christian Interpretation of the Cabbala in the Renaissance*, New York, 1944.

BROWN, PETER, *Augustine of Hippo*, London, 1967.

CASPAR, MAX, *John Kepler*, New York, 1960.

CORNFORD, F. M., *Plato's Cosmology*, London, 1937.

—— 'Mysticism and science in the Pythagorean Tradition', *Class. Q.*, XVII, 1923.

FINNEY, G. L., *Musical Backgrounds for English Literature*, New Brunswick, 1961.

FOWLER, ALASTAIR, D. S., *Spenser and the Numbers of Time*, London, 1964.

FREEMAN, KATHLEEN, *The Presocratic Philosophers*, Oxford, 1946.

GARIN, E., *Studi sul platonismo medioevo*, Florence, 1958.

GILBERT, STUART, *James Joyce's Ulysses*, Harmondsworth, 1963.

GUTHRIE, W. K. C., *History of Greek Philosophy*, I, Cambridge, 1962.

HACKFORTH, R., *Plato's Examination of Pleasure*, Cambridge, 1958.

HARRÉ, ROM., *The Anticipation of Nature*, London, 1965.

HART, CLIVE, *Structure and Motive in Finnegans Wake*, London, 1962.

HENINGER, S. K., 'Some Renaissance Versions of the Pythagorean Tetrad', *Studies in the Renaissance*, VIII, 1961.

HIEATT, KENT, *Short Time's Endless Monument*, New York, 1960.

HOPPER, VINCENT FOSTER, *Medieval Number Symbolism*, New York, 1938.

JOHNSON, F. R., *Astronomical Thought in Renaissance England*, Baltimore, 1937.

JUNG, CARL GUSTAV, *Psychology and Religion*, Yale, 1938.

KLIBANSKY, RAYMOND, *The Continuity of the Platonic Tradition*, London, Warburg Institute, 1939.

KLINE, MORRIS, *Mathematics in Western Culture*, Oxford, 1953.

KRISTELLER, O. P., *Renaissance Thought, I and II*, New York, Evanston and London, 1961 and 1965.

KUHN, THOMAS S., *The Copernican Revolution*, New York, 1959.

LE CORBUSIER, *The Modulor*, 1 and 2, London, 1954 and 1958.

MAZZEO, JOHN ANTONY, *Renaissance and Seventeenth Century Studies*, London, 1964.

NICOLSON, MARJORIE H., *The Breaking of the Circle*, New York, 1960.

PANOFSKY, ERWIN, *Meaning in the Visual Arts*, New York, 1955.

QUARNSTROM, GUNNAR, *Poetry and Numbers*, Lund, 1966.

REDLICH, H. F., *Alban Berg, the Man and his Music*, London, 1957.

RØSTVIG, MAREN-SOFIE, 'The Hidden Sense: Milton and the

Neoplatonic method of Numerical Composition', in *The Hidden Sense and other Essays*, Norwegian Studies in English, No. 9, Oslo and London, 1963.

SCHOLFIELD, P. H., *The Theory of Proportion in Architecture*, Cambridge, 1958.

SIMSON, OTTO VON, *The Gothic Cathedral*, New York, 1956.

SMALLEY, BERYL, *The Study of the Bible in the Middle Ages*, Oxford, 1941.

SPAETH, SIGMUND, *Milton's Knowledge of Music*, Michigan, 1963.

SPITZER, LEO, *Classical and Christian Ideas of World Harmony*, ed. Anna Granville Thatcher, Baltimore, 1963.

WALKER, D. P., *Spiritual and Demonic Magic from Ficino to Campanella*, London, Warburg Institute, 1958.

WITTKOWER, RUDOLF, *Architectural Principles in the Age of Humanism*, rev. ed., London, 1962.

YATES, FRANCES, *French Academies of the Sixteenth Century*, London, Warburg Institute, 1947.

—— *Giordano Bruno and the Hermetic Tradition*, London, 1964.

Index